THE FAMILY OF MANN

A Comedy in Two Acts

by Theresa Rebeck

SAMUEL FRENCH, INC.

45 WEST 25TH STREET   NEW YORK 10010
7623 SUNSET BOULEVARD   HOLLYWOOD 90046
LONDON   *TORONTO*

IMPORTANT BILLING AND CREDIT REQUIREMENTS

All producers of THE FAMILY OF MANN *must* give credit to the Author of the Play in all programs distributed in connection with performances of the Play and in all instances in which the title of the Play appears for purposes of advertising, publicizing or otherwise exploiting the Play and/or a production. The name of the Author *must* also appear on a separate line, on which no other name appears, immediately following the title, and *must* appear in size of type not less than fifty percent the size of the title type.

In addition, the following credit must be given in all programs distributed in connection with performances of the Play and in all advertising, publicizing or otherwise exploiting the Play and/or a production:

World Premiere Production by
The Second Stage Theatre, June 28, 1994
Artistic Director: Carole Rothman
Producing Dirctor: Suzanne Schwartz Davidson

The foregoing credit shall be of a size and prominence no smaller than the smallest creative element on such program title page or in such advertising and billings.

The Family of Mann premiered on June 28, 1994 at the Second Stage Theatre. It was directed by Pamela Berlin and had the following cast (in order of appearance):

ED/DAVE------------------------------David Garrison
BILL -------------------------------------Richard Cox
BELINDA/SISSY -------------------------Julie White
CLARA -------------------------- Lisa Gay Hamilton
REN/BUDDY--------------Robert Duncan McNeill
SALLY/GINNY --------------------------Anne Lange
STEVE/UNCLE WILLY -------------- Reed Birney

Scenic Designer: Derek McLane
Lighting Designer: Natasha Katz
Costume Designer: Lindsay W. Davis
Original Music & Sound Design: Jeremy Dyman Grody
Production Stage Manager: James Fitzsimmons

CHARACTERS

ED – the Executive Producer, mid-40s, large, friendly, a king.

REN – 31, boyish, good looking, likable.

BELINDA – 31, smart, opinionated, extremely emotional.

BILL – mid-40s, the director; a hatchet man.

SALLY – early 40s, feminine but determined.

STEVE – mid-40s, a fierce has been.

CLARA mid-20s, black, deferential but observant.

THE SIT COM

DAVE	Played by Ed
GINNY	Played by Sally
BUDDY	Played by Ren
SISSY	Played by Belinda
UNCLE WILLY	Played by Steve

The actress playing CLARA grows wings in the second act. Although no one comments on them, she should wear them in every scene.

TIME & PLACE

The Present. Los Angeles.

5

ACT I

Scene 1

FIRST READ THROUGH

The LIGHTS come up, bright on an ambiguous space. ED sits at a large table, EVERYONE else slightly behind him. EVERYONE holds script binders in their hands.

ED. Before we read through today's script, I just wanted to take a moment to welcome our actors, our production personnel, our talented staff of writers—all of you—to *The Family of Mann.* I think we're all excited to be here today, embarking on a project which will hopefully say something we can all be proud of, and maybe give us all a couple of laughs in the bargain, since that's what we're being paid for.

(HE laughs easily. EVERYONE else does too.)

ED. If you've seen any of the other shows we've worked on here, hopefully you realize that what we're trying to do is quality television that people can watch without being completely, egregiously offended morally and intellectually. It's a crazy idea, but we like to kid ourselves that stories about people living relatively decent, normal lives, the kind of lives I think most of us had in our childhood, might be of interest to America. Anyway, it's of interest to me, and I've had some success with this approach, so we're going to try it again and see if we can prove to the networks that Americans are not merely interested in amoral, sex-crazed psychopaths, or whatever it is they're putting on the air this week. Now, before we get started, I want to explain a few things about our organization. We really do consider ourselves a family here; mostly what we're interested in is creating a world where people can just enjoy coming in to work. If it's not fun, then I'm not interested in it, and I don't think you should be either. So I hope we can all just relax and enjoy each other and make some comedy here! (*There is scattered applause.*) I give you our director, Bill.

(*EVERYONE holds pencils and opens identical scripts. BILL, the director, starts to read.*)

BILL. Okay, here we are in the Mann family kitchen. It's a Saturday morning, the day is bright and lovely and Ginny, the lovely wife of Dave Mann, is talking to her husband. Scene one.

(*LIGHTS change.*)

Scene 2

Belinda: THE WRITERS' ROOM

Scene changes to the writers' room. All the WRITERS sit around the table, scripts open before them. EVERYONE speaks very quickly.

ED. He's as big as a fucking cow. I mean, the last time I saw him was at the pilot, he looks great, and today, what, he's put on thirty pounds in two months.

SALLY. I put a call into his agent.

ED. Fuck his fucking agent. The man's old enough to know when he looks like a pig. Fucking actors. I can't believe this. He gets paid sixty thousand dollars a week to stay in shape and he shows up looking like Orson Welles.

REN. We have the same lawyer, I had lunch with him last week? First thing he says, so, how much weight has Jim put on? His last show, every hiatus he put on thirty pounds. Apparently he does this all the time.

ED. Oh, Jesus. (*To Sally.*) Did you know about this?

SALLY. Of course not—

BELINDA. I don't think he looks bad—

ED. You put a camera on him, he's a mess. Six months ago, the guy is America's perfect father. This is making me sick. Get his agent on the phone.

(SALLY picks up the phone.)

SALLY. (*Into phone.*) Clara, can you get Andrew Stein for me, please? (*SHE hangs up.*)

STEVE. (*Overlap.*) The script's in good shape.

ED. The script's phenomenal. As long as Jim doesn't sit on it.

(BILL enters as the PHONE rings. SALLY picks it up and speaks while BILL and ED speak.)

ED. How's it going?

BILL. Fine, except for the fact that Jim is as big as a fucking house.

SALLY. (*Overlap.*) Andy? Oh, wonderful. Yes, it went very well; everyone's very excited. The network is very happy. Listen, Andy, we're a little concerned about Jim's weight.

ED. Could you believe it when he walked in? The guy's supposed to be our leading man, his gut is hanging over his—

BILL. And he's eating donuts, he doesn't pass the fucking table without picking up something, I think he's already had four or five.

ED. Jesus.

SALLY. (*Overlap.*) So he is aware of it?

BILL. He's stuffing himself.

SALLY. Well, Ed's not sure—here, let me have you talk to Ed—

ED. Fuck him, I don't want to talk to some fucking agent. I want to talk to his trainer. If he's so fucking aware of it, how come he's still fat? The guy's being paid sixty thousand dollars a week to stay thin—

SALLY. (*Into phone, overlap.*) Andy, we just wanted to make sure something was being done. Is he seeing a trainer, or—oh, good, good. So you'll tell him that we are concerned? Good. Okay. (*SHE hangs up.*)

BILL. I've seen this before. This is bad, this is fear of success. You can't start like this; if you don't come out of the gate like a fucking maniac it's all over.

BELINDA. I don't think he looks bad. He's incredibly appealing. My mother has the hugest crush on—

ED. Oh, Jesus, I feel sick. Can we get some lunch menus in here?

(SALLY picks up the phone again.)

BILL. *(Overlap, to Belinda.)* You don't understand; you can't start like this. If you start like this, it's all over. He's sabotaging the whole show.

ED. I didn't want to cast him in the first place. The guy looks like a weasel. Now he looks like a fat weasel.

(HE and BILL laugh.)

SALLY. Clara, can you bring the lunch menus in? Thanks. *(SHE hangs up.)*

ED. Fuck him. The script's phenomenal; it's going to be a great show. We'll just keep the camera on Monica all week, is she a beautiful girl or what?

REN. She has the most beautiful skin of any girl I have ever seen. She glows. She actually glows.

ED. What a punim. She good?

BILL. Unbelievable.

ED. Terrific.

CLARA. *(Enters with a book of menus.)* You guys ready to order lunch?

ED. Skip the menus, do we need to see menus? Just pick up a bunch of pizzas. Six or seven, I don't care. Jesus, this is making me—and stop off at Victor's for chocolate cake. We'll sit here and stuff our faces and make fun of how fat Jim is.

(HE and BILL laugh. BLACKOUT.)

Scene 3

Ed: THE FAMILY OF MANN I

A suburban kitchen. DAD sits at a table, reading the newspaper while MOM chatters. THEY perform in a bright, skittish, sitcom style.

GINNY. Maybe I'll write a novel today.

(DAD gives her a look. The LAUGH TRACK chuckles.)

DAVE. You're going to write a novel, today? What are you going to write tomorrow, an encyclopedia?

(More laughter.)

GINNY. I mean it, Dave. I want to do something *big* today.

DAVE. How about we paint the living room?

(More laughter. SHE glares at him.)

DAVE. What? we have a very large living room!

(More laughter.)

GINNY. Dave, we're finally free! We could do anything! We could travel or go back to school, or learn how to ski!

DAVE. Go bungee jumping.

GINNY. Anything! Now that the kids have finally moved out, I feel so energized! Dave. We finally got rid of them.

(More laughter.)

DAVE. You sound like you hate your own children.

GINNY. No, hate would be too strong a word. Or maybe it wouldn't ...

(More laughter.)

DAVE. Ginny!

GINNY. Dave, now that they're adults, it's time we faced facts. We have the most annoying children in America.

DAVE. I like them!

GINNY. I like them too, when they're not driving me crazy. Twenty-two years of "Mom, it's your day for car pool." "Mom, will you press my new blouse?" "Mom—"

BUDDY. *(Off.)* Mom, what's for breakfast?

GINNY. *(To Dad.)* Yes, I especially hated that one. Mom, what's for breakfast? In that annoying nasal twang Buddy has. You sounded just like him for a second there.

BUDDY. *(Entering.)* Mooooom! What's for breaaaaakfast?

GINNY. *(Laughing.)* Oh, stop! How do you do that?

(DAD stares at her. SHE gets it, leaping to her feet.)

GINNY. Buddy! What are you doing here?

BUDDY. I thought I'd come by for breakfast.

(HE sits, expectant. MOM is confused.)

GINNY. You live in Chicago, sweetheart. Why would you come all the way to Minneapolis to have breakfast?

BUDDY. Well, see, there's this little thing called a recession, Mom. Could I have some orange juice?

(More laughter. SHE stares at him.)

SISSY. *(Off.)* Moooooom!

(MOM turns, desperate.)

GINNY. Sissy!

(SISSY enters, weeping, and throws herself on Mom's shoulder.)

SISSY. It's so awful—oh, Mom—

GINNY. What is it, sweetheart, what's the matter?

SISSY. My husband is the most hateful man that ever lived.

GINNY. *(Sympathetic.)* We've all known that for years, sweetheart. Why are you crying?

(More laughter.)

SISSY. Can I stay here, Mom?

BUDDY. Mom, I lost my job and my apartment, and I'm broke. It's okay if I stay here, isn't it?

GINNY. Oh, my poor sweet babies. I'd rather stick my fingers in a waffle iron than let you move back home.

(More laughter. Beat.)

SISSY and BUDDY. Daddy?
DAVE. Oh, she's kidding. Of course you can stay! Isn't this great. We're a family again!

(HE puts his arms around Buddy and Sissy. After a moment, GINNY makes a running jump and leaps on Sissy, trying to strangle her. ALL try to pry them apart. Laughter and applause. BLACKOUT.)

Scene 4

Bill: IT'S NOT REAL ENOUGH

The writers' room. EVERYONE is sitting around the table. There is food and Coke cans everywhere.

ED. This doesn't, it just doesn't start right.
STEVE. Well, we talked about her, you know, her feeling of liberation when—
ED. Yeah, but a novel, it's too literary, everyone in America's going to be going who are these fucking people, writing novels, it's not real—
BELINDA. My mother tried to write a novel once.

ED. (*Not listening.*) That's the mistake everybody makes, like all this sniping at each other, that's not real. Once you give into that sort of shit, you're dead.

STEVE. Well, we don't have to start with the novel, I just thought it would give a sense of her, you know—

ED. Yeah, but it's got to be real. This show is—we're bringing the family together in adulthood, now, we're showing Americans moving out of their adolescence into a deeper maturity.

BILL. I think we should start with Sissy and Buddy, that's where the heat is going to be. Either one of them could be a breakout. I say we just start with the heat.

REN. What, do you mean open with them already there?

BILL. Yeah, some sort of funny scene with the two of them plotting to get their old rooms back or something.

REN. Except he's after her room. Just getting back in the house isn't enough, he's—

ED. You mean, she's got the room with the view of Minneapolis?

REN. Something like that. A spectacular view of downtown Minneapolis, and he's after that room.

SALLY. Ren, that is a great idea.

BELINDA. So they get into some totally moronic juvenile fight about it? That could work. I mean, they start out as children and then—

ED. Yeah, but it's still—there's something not right about the tone. These people should not be mean to each other. They tease each other, but without meanness.

BELINDA. Well, if we started with the brother sister thing we would lose the section where Dave picks on Ginny, that's where I thought it was sounding kind of—

ED. No, that part's okay. It was the stuff about her not liking her kids that I thought really went too far.

BILL. The attitudes are reversed. Dave should be the one who doesn't want the kids back; that's where the comedy is. She's gotta be thrilled to see them.

ED. Yeah, this stuff about not liking her kids doesn't work.

BELINDA. (*Cheerful.*) Well, I don't know. My mother hated me all the time. Didn't your mother hate you?

ED. No, I don't think—you're very nosey. Is this why your mother hated you?

BELINDA. It was just a periodic thing. You know, when you date drug addicts and come home trashed, parents tend to get upset. And isn't that like what we're going for with these two, that they're both—

ED. No, they're good kids, they aren't—

BELINDA. Well, I was a good kid too. I was just a good kid who got arrested a couple times. (*SHE laughs.*)

REN. You got arrested?

BELINDA. Oh, for buying cocaine. Big deal. I was a minor. It's not like I have a record or anything.

ED. Well, that's a big relief. You were buying drugs, but you were underage. I feel much better.

BELINDA. So, let's give Sissy a drug phase.

STEVE. Drugs aren't funny.

BELINDA. They're not?

ED. These are good kids. They're not drug addicts.

SALLY. Maybe if the opening is just more about Ginny's realizing the kids are gone—

ED. I need more coffee. CLARA! Is there coffee? CLARA!

CLARA. *(Enters.)* I'm in the next room, Ed. You don't have to roar.

ED. We need coffee.

SALLY. *(Overlap.)* She doesn't know what to do with herself ...

CLARA. I just made a pot fifteen minutes ago. (*SHE picks it up and looks at it, pours it into his cup.*)

ED. Oh, this is fresh? I didn't know this was fresh.

SALLY. *(Overlap.)* There's a sense of confusion and loss—

ED. Oh yeah, those confusion and loss jokes are always such a scream.

(The GUYS laugh.)

SALLY. No, I mean, if we tried to play it comedically—

ED. Comedically. Ohhhh. Now, everything is clear. (*Off coffee.*) This stuff is phenomenal. How do you make this?

CLARA. Well, you put the little white filter in the machine. Then you open the little silver bag and pour the coffee in.

ED. Phenomenal.

CLARA. I can't believe they pay you so much and me so little.

ED. I adore this girl.

BILL. Could I have some of that?

(BILL holds out his cup. As CLARA pours, HE puts his arm around her.)

ED. She's phenomenal, isn't she?

BILL. Fantastic.

ED. So what do we have? Comedic confusion and loss.

BILL. I just think we gotta be careful not to lose Dave in all this. What I want to know is where Dave is.

ED. As played by Jim, Dave is standing in the corner with his fist up his ass.

(The GUYS all laugh.)

REN. Sitcom for the nineties. *(Doing Jackie Gleason.)* "Norton! How would you like my fist up your ass?"

(The GUYS howl.)

BILL. "Alice! Why, I oughta just shove my fist up Norton's ass!"

REN. *(As Alice.)* "You do whatever you want, Ralph. Trixie and I are going to go lick each other dry."

STEVE. *(As Norton.)* "Hey, Ralph, Ralpheroonie, the girls are going to ... lick each other dry! Don't you think we should, uh ... watch?"

REN. *(As Alice.)* "Why that's a great idea, Norton. You coming, Ralph?"

BILL. "Alice ... you're the greatest."

(THEY are laughing uproariously. BELINDA watches, puzzled, and SALLY smiles politely. CLARA does not respond.)

BILL. Oh, God. Oh, God ...

REN. *(As Ralph.)* "Norton!"

(THEY all laugh even harder.)

ED. So what do we have, Dave is standing around with Norton's fist up his ass? Well, at least it's funny.

(THEY continue to laugh. LIGHTS change.)

Scene 5

Belinda: REALITY

ED and BELINDA are in his office.

ED. You like it here? I mean, everything's going okay? Need anything?

BELINDA. No, it's great. Everything's great.

ED. It's an amazing job, isn't it? I mean, the first show I got, I thought, they have to be kidding. I couldn't imagine how anybody would be willing to pay me for this. They put me in a room with three other guys and said, all right, entertain yourselves all day, eat as much as you like, and while you're at it, if you write a few things down, we'll put them on television for you. Oh, and by the way, we'll pay you a zillion dollars for this. It's like stealing money.

BELINDA. It's pretty amazing. I mean, it seems—I'm still getting used to it, but, you know—I'm writing for a TV show! I'm sorry, I'm sounding like a moron—

ED. No, no—

BELINDA. Anyway, thank you for the opportunity. And, I hope I wasn't crossing lines in there, with the drug stuff—

ED. Not at all.

BELINDA. I just thought that might be an area for comedy, so I was—

ED. You'll figure it out.

BELINDA. I just, you know, I'm real excited about being here, so I want to do a good job, and I get—anyway. And on top of it all, to be making so much money, I—

ED. No, you can't do it for the money. That's the first mistake everybody makes. If you do it for the money, you're lost. If it's there, if it's not there, you have to be the same person.

BELINDA. (*Laughing a little.*) Well, some day I hope to be the same person with a lot more money.

ED. You need money?

BELINDA. Oh. No, that's not—I'm fine. I'm doing fine. Thank you.

ED. I mean, the money's good. It's a good thing. To be able to support your family, and take care of the people you love. You don't have that worry right now, but you will. But for now, it's good that you can just learn the craft, and enjoy the opportunity. Television is so powerful; there's no other form of entertainment that reaches so many people. That's what's so great about what we do. We make a difference. We literally affect people's lives.

BELINDA. It's quite a responsibility.

ED. You're a talented girl. You're going to do fine out here. Los Angeles takes a little getting used to, but really, it's a wonderful place. It's possibly the last great cauldron of the American character, do you know what I mean?

We're creating a landscape, creating an art form, creating ourselves. It's the essence of America. That's what I like most about Los Angeles. It allows you to create your own reality.

BELINDA. Oh. But—wow. I don't know. If you create it, is it real? I mean, I thought we were creating fantasies.

(SHE laughs, friendly. HE stares at her. LIGHTS change.)

Scene 6

Ed: DID YOU SEE MY NAME?

BELINDA is at home. SHE is lit by the BLUE LIGHT of a television set. SHE is talking on the phone and drinking a beer.

BELINDA. (*On phone, excited.*) Did you see it? Did you see my name? (*SHE laughs.*) I know, it was wild, wasn't it? Did Grandma like it? (*Pause.*) She thought it was too *racy*? Well, what do you want, she's near death, everything's racy to her. Mom. I'm kidding, Mom. Hi, Daddy! Yeah, it was great wasn't it? Well, not great, but for my first episode on television—yeah, it was exciting. It looked so *real*. And it's so weird, because that's *not* real, you know, but there it is on the television screen, and it's like, man, it's like you exist. It's so ... Dad? Oh. Hi, Gigi! Yeah, it was great, wasn't it? Uh huh. Uh huh. No, I didn't write that, I didn't write that part. Well, you know, as a group, we rewrite things, and—(*Pause.*) No, I—I

didn't write that, either. Yeah, Ed wrote that. (*Pause*.)
Yeah, I wrote some of it—(*Lying*.) yeah, I wrote that. That
was my line. Good, yeah, I—Uh ... who is this? Mrs.
Markgraf! Yeah, it is fun being in Hollywood. No, uh, no
I—I haven't met Tom Cruise. Could you put my dad back
on? Thanks. (*Pause, laughing*.) Dad, how many people are
there? Well, yeah, but—of course I did. I had a, a bunch of
friends came over and we watched it together. They're in
the other room. Okay, you go back to your party and I'll
go back to mine. Yeah. I love you too. 'Bye. (*SHE hangs
up. Beat. Calling to no one*.) Be right there. (*Beat*.) I'm
sooo pathetic.

(*LIGHTS change*.)

Scene 7

Belinda: PHENOMENAL

ED and BILL are in Ed's office.

ED. You see the reviews?

BILL. Phenomenal. We're gold.

ED. I can't believe it. You see *The New York Times*?
The network guys, they're telling me they've never seen
reviews like this. Not since *All in the Family*.

BILL. It just goes to show, people are hungry.

ED. Yeah, but now we gotta hit a home run every
week. We gotta keep the heat on until we see what the
numbers look like.

BILL. I'm not kidding, this is it, Ed. This is the way I felt the first week of *Family Business*. When it works, it works. We're going seven years.

ED. You think so?

BILL. If Jim goes on a diet.

ED. Fuck him. He can lose the weight or he's out of here. This isn't fucking *Designing Women*, or *Rosanne*, for that matter. Anybody can be replaced. Just make sure he knows that.

BILL. No, he's fine, he's going to the gym, he's going to be—

ED. Is he pulling anything? Come late to rehearsals or anything?

BILL. No, he's scared to death. He's desperate for this show to survive; he's got something like four mortgages to pay off. He's not going to fuck up.

ED. Is that why he's doing all those fried chicken commercials?

BILL. I guess.

ED. Jesus.

BILL. How's the table?

ED. Great. I mean, I'm still not sure this is Steve's kind of show, and Sally's not—you know, we're stuck with her, what are you going to do? They're friends; no one else will give them jobs. But Ren and Belinda are phenomenal. You read their scripts?

BILL. Phenomenal.

ED. First time out for both of them. Unbelievable.

BILL. Where'd you find her?

ED. In a stack. I mean, her spec came in over the fucking transom, I don't even know why I read it. I just pulled it out of a stack one day on a whim, and I thought, fuck, this is good, let's just hire her. She's got a fucking Ph.D., did you know that?

BILL. You're shitting me.

ED. Taught English at some university and got sick of it. I'm going to call fucking Cosby and say, fuck you and your Ph.D. I got a *story* editor with a Ph.D., take that and shove it up your ass.

BILL. (*Laughing.*) That's perfect. You should, you should do it.

ED. Fucking Cosby and his fucking Ph.D. Anyway, I read her script, and I think, you know, she's good, and then that afternoon, I go to this psychic, who tells me, out of the blue, that a woman named Linda is going to come into my life and make a huge impact.

BILL. Linda?

ED. Is that amazing? I mean, it's not exactly the same, but—

BILL. No, but—you didn't—

ED. Nothing. I was there to ask about whether or not I should buy another house, Deb and I are thinking about buying a place in Santa Monica because the beach house is so far, and there are so many people at the house in Brentwood all the time we can't be alone, with the gardener, and the housekeeper and Becky and the kids—

BILL. Yeah, yeah—

ED. So I hadn't said anything about hiring writers. I mean, we weren't even sure the show was going at that point.

BILL. That's wild.

ED. Yeah. A woman named "Linda." And what about Ren, he remind you of anybody?

(BILL looks at him, actively thinking.)

ED. Me! Doesn't he remind you of me? About twenty years ago?

BILL. Oh—

ED. Yeah, I went back to that psychic today, to talk about the show, and you know what she told me? That I was going to have a son. Out of the blue, she says, I see a son coming into your life. A prince among men. And, you know, Deb's forty-six, she's not—

BILL. Well, you never—

ED. I know, but be realistic. I mean, with these psychics, you can't always be literal. She says a son, but that might mean a lot of things. So when I got back to the lot today, I bumped into Ren, and I thought: This is what she was talking about. A prince. Of course, I didn't know that when I hired him. This just happened today.

BILL. Ren's great. His script is phenomenal.

ED. And what a jump shot. Did you see him yesterday, making that shot from the corner?

BILL. See him? I was trying to stop him. I'm going, all of a sudden he's Michael Jordan—

ED. He played college ball.

BILL. You're shitting me.

ED. You didn't know? He made it to the Final Four. Twice.

BILL. Jesus.

ED. That's why I hired him.

(THEY laugh. LIGHTS change.)

. Scene 8

Ren: THE NUMBERS

REN and STEVE and BELINDA are in the writers' room. CLARA enters, carrying yellow sheets of paper.

CLARA. The numbers came in.

(STEVE and REN jump, take the sheets eagerly.)

STEVE. All of them?
CLARA. Just the overnights. We won our slot.
REN. All right! (*HE gives Clara a high-five.*)
STEVE. (*Studying sheet.*) Not by much. Jesus. Not by much at all. A tenth of a point.
BELINDA. Now how do you read these?
REN. (*Pointing.*) This number is the percentage of available sets that were tuned into our show, and this one is—percentage of viewers. Of the sets that were turned on, this is how many watched us.
BELINDA. What?
STEVE. This is not good at all.
CLARA. Bill says we'll bounce in the nationals.
STEVE. You didn't take these down to the set, did you?
CLARA. No, he came by before he went over—
STEVE. Never let an actor see a number. It makes them completely insane.

(ED and SALLY enter. SHE is trying to show him Polaroids.)

SALLY. You can't tell from the Polaroids, Ed. We have to go over there. It'll take ten minutes—

ED. I told you; I don't care what they wear.

SALLY. You say that, and then on show night all of a sudden nobody looks right—

CLARA. The numbers came in. (*SHE hands sheets to Sally and Ed.*)

SALLY. Oh, no. We fell four points off our lead.

STEVE. That fucking black show is a piece of shit, and then they blame us because everybody turns it off in the middle.

ED. It doesn't matter. Those assholes at the network will do whatever they want anyway. You have to ignore this shit. Is there coffee?

CLARA. What's the magic word?

ED. Clara, my love, is there coffee?

CLARA. Ed, sweetie, for you, there's always coffee. (*SHE goes to get it.*)

SALLY. I love your shirt, Ren. That's a terrific color on you.

REN. Thanks.

SALLY. All right, I'm going to wardrobe. I'll be back in ten minutes; don't start without me. (*SHE goes.*)

BELINDA. (*Still trying to figure it out.*) This number is the percentage of what?...

ED. You can't pay any attention to them. Jesus, these numbers are for shit. Steve, look at what *Empty Nest* did, and that's a fucking hit.

STEVE. Back in the eighties, no one could stay on with these numbers.

ED. The networks are going down. Fuck 'em, they deserve to; they're as bad as the car companies. They put shit on year after year, it serves them right that people finally won't watch it. Shit, I don't want to talk about the numbers. Belinda, how's your script coming?

BELINDA. I'm proofing it over lunch. You'll have it this afternoon.

ED. Great. Did you put in that stuff we talked about? About Dave interfering with Sissy's boyfriends?

BELINDA. Yeah. It's a little creepy, but I think I figured out how to make it work.

ED. Creepy?

BELINDA. Ed, she's twenty-nine years old and her father won't let her date.

ED. So, what's your point? (*HE laughs.*)

BELINDA. Right. So, I put that in and moved the dog food run to the top of the D scene; it's much hotter there—

ED. Great—

BELINDA. And I cut four pages out of the second act and reconceived Jimmy.

ED. Jimmy? I liked Jimmy.

BELINDA. He wasn't funny enough.

ED. Is he funny now?

BELINDA. This guy is so funny, he makes Robin Williams look like a big bore.

ED. You think Williams is funny?

BELINDA. Not as funny as you, Ed.

ED. I love this girl.

BELINDA. Yeah, yeah, yeah ... (*SHE goes.*)

ED. (*To Ren.*) She's great, isn't she? She's a machine. How's your new script coming?

REN. Great. You'll have it by the end of the week.

ED. She's gaining on you.

(ED laughs. REN laughs with him, sort of.)

STEVE. Ed, I probably should get going on a second script, too. I mean, I haven't really done much since that first script and I have a couple ideas.

ED. Oh, well, yeah, sure Steve. Put them together and we'll talk.

STEVE. Well, is now a good time? I could pitch 'em now. It shouldn't take too long.

ED. *(Looking at the sheets again.)* No, why don't you hold onto them for a few days. Now is not really a great time.

STEVE. Oh. Okay.

ED. Fucking numbers. Ren, you want to go do some editing?

REN. Sure.

ED. Your episode is looking phenomenal. We just have to get another thirty seconds out of it.

REN. Great.

(THEY go. STEVE sits alone for a long moment. SALLY enters. SHE looks around.)

SALLY. Where is everybody? I thought we were working.

(STEVE looks at her. LIGHTS change.)

Scene 9

Sally: THE BEST PLACE TO WORK IN HOLLYWOOD

SALLY arranges flowers on her desk. There is also a teapot and cups. BELINDA looks around.

BELINDA. What a lovely office.

SALLY. Thank you. I like to keep it pretty, so there's at least one place on the lot I can come to for a little—comfort, I suppose. Would you like some tea?

BELINDA. Oh, sure, that'd be great.

(SALLY pours and hands her a cup.)

SALLY. So, how are you liking it here?

BELINDA. Well, you know, it's great, I just, a lot, it's real different.

SALLY. From the university?

BELINDA. Well, from anything, as far as I can tell. (*Pause.*) I didn't know you knew about the whole ... university thing.

SALLY. Oh, I'm sorry. Was it a secret?

BELINDA. No, of course not. I just—actually, I did ask Ed not to mention it. He found out about it through my agent, I didn't—

SALLY. Oh, Ed's telling everyone. You should be proud. It's quite an accomplishment.

BELINDA. Thank you. I just didn't want people to think I was an intellectual snob, or anything.

SALLY. Not at all. Well. A drug phase and a Ph.D. You're a very interesting person, aren't you?

BELINDA. It was a very small drug phase, I don't know why I even—

SALLY. You must miss teaching. (*SHE hands her a cup of tea.*)

BELINDA. Well, yeah, I guess I do. There actually was something really comforting about discussing Victorian novels for twelve hours a day.

SALLY. I'm sure it was a much more intellectual environment.

BELINDA. Oh, no—I mean, yes, of course, but—

SALLY. We read too.

BELINDA. Oh, I know. I didn't—I really don't miss it that much. I was constantly broke and the politics—I didn't actually fit in.

SALLY. Oh, no. You're lovely! I'm sure you fit in everywhere you go.

BELINDA. Well, thank you. But I never actually felt comfortable as an academic. I mean, I loved teaching, but the faculty ... I felt like this populist in elitist heaven. I prefer Dickens to Henry James.

SALLY. Really.

BELINDA. Yeah. And I just thought, writing for television, if Dickens were alive today, that's where he'd be, so—

SALLY. Well, you're very lucky to be with us on your first show. This is one of the best places to work in Hollywood. Ed is one of the few truly decent and supportive people in the industry, and he really does want you to consider this a home. You're lucky.

BELINDA. (*Cautious.*) Everyone's been great. And I really am thrilled to be here.

SALLY. Well, good.

BELINDA. Of course, it's pretty different than I thought it would be. I guess I thought it was going to be sort of like the *Dick Van Dyke Show*, and, you know, it's really not.

SALLY. It does get a little rough sometimes. You must find that hard, coming from your ivory tower.

BELINDA. Oh, no. I love three hours of fist up the ass jokes. We used to kid about that all the time back at the old ivory tower. In between all the drugs we did.

(SALLY looks at her. BELINDA laughs. After a moment, SALLY laughs back.)

SALLY. My first job, on *Happy Days*, the first day I was there, one of the other writers unzipped his pants, put his cock on the table and told me to suck it.

(Pause.)

BELINDA. You're kidding.

SALLY. I was the only woman in a room of ten. They all thought it was hilarious, of course. I was twenty-four years old.

BELINDA. What did you do?

SALLY. Well, I certainly didn't oblige him. I laughed in a slightly uncomfortable way. (*SHE demonstrates.*) After a month or so the joke wore thin and he went on to something else. The whole trick is going along with it, but not really. You know.

BELINDA. I don't think I do.

SALLY. You can't protest, because that would get in the way of the room's energy, but you also can't just pretend that you're one of them. Because, we're not. Are we?

BELINDA. Apparently not.

SALLY. Anyway, you don't have to worry about the really overt stuff here. Ed wouldn't tolerate it.

BELINDA. He wouldn't.

SALLY. Absolutely not. He's actually rather traditional.

BELINDA. Traditional?

SALLY. On the last season of *Family Business*, we had a staff writer, a woman, who told the filthiest jokes in the room. She also tried to play basketball with them in one of their pickup games. She didn't last the season.

BELINDA. (*Pause.*) Are you warning me about something?

SALLY. I'm just trying to help. Ed is a complicated person. I hope you understand that.

BELINDA. You're kind of complicated yourself, aren't you?

SALLY. Not really. All I want out of life is to make a lot of money. More money than I can count. So much money that everyone will have to kiss up to me, and I can treat anyone I want like dirt. (*SHE laughs.*) More tea? (*SHE pours.*)

(*LIGHTS change.*)

Scene 10

Belinda: **THE FAMILY OF MANN II**

SISSY and BUDDY are reading a newspaper. SISSY is circling items. GINNY bustles about the kitchen.

SISSY. (*Wistful.*) I miss Benny.

BUDDY. Benny? The guy who chained you to the kitchen counter until you learned how to make a pie crust?

SISSY. That wasn't what it looked like.

BUDDY. It looked like about sixty pounds of wrought iron.

(Laugh track.)

SISSY. You never liked him.

BUDDY. Well, no I didn't. And now that I find out he's been married to another woman the whole time he was married to you, I like him even less.

SISSY. Nobody's perfect!

(More laughter.)

BUDDY. I know nobody's perfect, but Benny isn't even in the ball park! Why are you defending him?

SISSY. I just think that everyone has a good side, that's all.

BUDDY. Yeah, well, Benny's good side belongs in a federal penitentiary.

(More laughter.)

SISSY. What do you know about it?

(THEY start to argue. GINNY laughs.)

GINNY. Okay, you two! I don't want to have to separate you! (*Smiling.*) Kids ...

(More laughter. UNCLE WILLY and DAVE enter.)

DAVE. Hey! Look who I found!

SISSY. Uncle Willy!

UNCLE WILLY. I was in the neighborhood, thought I'd stop by, visit my favorite brother and his gorgeous wife. You look fabulous, Ginny.

GINNY. Thanks, Willy. Have you had lunch?

UNCLE WILLY. Lunch! That would be terrific. Lunch, dinner, whatever. Breakfast. A chance to visit with my favorite niece and nephew for a few hours. A couple of days, weeks, months. Whatever! I'll just settle in a corner somewhere; you can throw me a bone once in a while. Sissy! You look fabulous.

(Laughter.)

DAVE. (*Threatening.*) Willy ...

UNCLE WILLY. (*Begging.*) Just for a little while, Dave, till my trail cools off. I mean, till I get back on my feet!

DAVE. Alright. Everybody out! Not you, Willy!

(The OTHERS go. WILLY turns, desperate, to Dave.)

UNCLE WILLY. Dave. Dave, don't hit me, Dave. I'm not in a lot of trouble. A little, tiny misunderstanding with a loan shark.

DAVE. I'm sick, Willy. I just found out. I may be dying.

UNCLE WILLY. (*Pause.*) What?

DAVE. I don't know how to tell Ginny, or the kids. I know we haven't always gotten along, but—you are my brother. Can you help me?

(THEY hug. BLACKOUT.)

Scene 11

Ren: REAL MONEY

The writers' room. Exhausted, REN and BELINDA are going through a mass of orange pages, copy editing with a pencil. Periodically, THEY pass pages back and forth. THEY keep reading as THEY talk.

BELINDA. What time is it?

REN. It's a little after two.

BELINDA. Oh, fuck. Jesus, fuck me. Where's the rest of this scene? (*SHE paws dully through the pages.*)

REN. What is it?

BELINDA. G. G. G, G, G. I only have half of it.

REN. That's the whole scene.

BELINDA. It's not the whole scene. What happened to the part where he tells them he's not dying?

REN. That's there.

BELINDA. No, it's not.

(SHE hands the pages to him. REN reads.)

REN. Oh, shit. Did we cut that? *(HE starts pawing through the pages.)*

BELINDA. How could we cut it? The whole episode is about whether he's dying or not.

REN. Where is the old draft?

(THEY both are pawing through white pages by now.)

BELINDA. Fuck. Fuck me. We're going to be here all night. It's a good thing they pay us a fortune.

REN. My deal is fucked. I have a terrible deal. Ed is—I mean, he's a great guy, he's been great to me, but he's— you know, he's made a lot of promises that he doesn't keep. I was supposed to be a producer on this show.

BELINDA. Oh, yeah? And instead you're just a shitty little story editor like me.

REN. No, I mean, it's great being here, I'm just saying. I'm never going to make any real money here.

BELINDA. We're making four thousand dollars a week. That's not real money? What's real money?

REN. Four thousand dollars a week is not real money.

BELINDA. How did you end up here, anyway?

REN. My sister-in-law was a regular on *Family Business* the last season. She played the nun who tried to teach the twins to tap dance.

BELINDA. Oh, right. I missed that.

REN. So Ed and I got to know each other. We started playing basketball together.

BELINDA. Then you never did this before.

REN. Well, you know, I had a couple guest spots on *Who's the Boss?* and *Full House.* Here it is. Is this it? (*HE reads off of some pages.*) Dave says, "I just sat there and heard the doctor say, you don't have cancer. It's nothing. And then I thought, if it's nothing, how come you're charging me an arm and a leg?"

BELINDA. Oh, God, did we leave that terrible joke in there?

REN. Hey. I wrote that terrible joke.

BELINDA. Oh. I'm sorry—

REN. It's okay. It is a terrible joke. But it's two fifteen, and it's all we got. Where's the first half of the scene?

BELINDA. No, come on, we gotta fix it. I mean, there's got to be a way to fix this. (*SHE takes the page and stares at it.*)

REN. Belinda—

BELINDA. How about if we just take it out?

REN. Belinda.

BELINDA. (*Preoccupied, looking at the page.*) That'll work. Actually, this is moment that should not have a joke at all, rhythmically it doesn't— He's facing his mortality, I don't want to hear one-liners ... (*SHE starts to block out a cut on the page.*)

REN. We can't just change the script on our own! Ed is going to throw a fit—

BELINDA. Ed is gonna love this. Look, it clears out a moment for the two of them, and, you know, if we don't build an emotional context—

REN. An emotional *what*?

BELINDA. Look, just because it's a sitcom doesn't mean it has to be shit. This will make it better, so what's your problem?

REN. Well, excuse me. I mean, it's just my script. What would *I* know about it?

BELINDA. Ren, you said yourself it's a bad joke! Why are you fighting for it?

REN. Why are you fighting against it? It's two in the fucking morning!

CLARA. (*Staggers in.*) Are you guys okay?

BELINDA. Yeah.

CLARA. Are you almost done?

REN. Yes.

BELINDA. No.

CLARA. You know, we're not writing *The Brothers Karamazov* in here.

BELINDA. We're just working on a few ...

CLARA. Great. I'm gonna be here till three.

(SHE goes. REN stares at the pages, grim and exhausted.)

BELINDA. I'm sorry. I just, I taught writing for so long, you know, freshman comp, I spent so many years telling undergrads how important good writing is, and so many people watch television, I just keep having this vision in my head of all these people gathered around it like a campfire and we're the storytellers, and ... (*Pause.*) Never mind. We'll just leave it.

REN. No, take it out. You're right. It's better without it. It is.

BELINDA. I'm sorry, I didn't—

REN. It's fine.

(HE takes the pages from her and crosses the section out. SHE watches him.)

REN. Okay, Clara, we're done—

CLARA. *(Enters, yawning.)* Who won?

REN. Belinda.

BELINDA. It wasn't—

REN. Yes it was.

CLARA. Just don't start up again. Man, I'm tired ...

(SHE takes the pages as REN and BELINDA collect their things. Completely energetic, ED enters.)

ED. Hey! It's my two favorite writers! Clara, my love, is there coffee?

CLARA. It's two in the morning, Ed!

ED. So where is everybody? Are these the proofs? (*HE takes the proofs from Clara and starts to page through them.*)

CLARA. Oh, my god. Maybe if I drove a stake through his heart ...

ED. I love this girl.

CLARA. I'll go make coffee ...

BELINDA. Ed—we didn't know you were still here.

ED. I've been over in editing. So, what, are you quitting? Deadbeats. Nobody's got any stamina anymore. My first season in television, I worked with three guys who never went home. I mean, literally. We'd work until four every night, then they'd go back and sleep in their offices. I didn't have an office, so I had to drive to Santa Monica, and back three hours later. My marriage was the only one that survived the season ... (*Reading*.) Whoa, you lost the arm and a leg joke?

BELINDA. Oh—

REN. I just thought, you know, he's facing his mortality, we don't need to hear one-liners. And it gives the scene a little more room so that there's an emotional context. For the characters.

ED. An emotional context? He's sounding like a real writer, isn't he? It's a great script, Ren ... (*HE chuckles, looking at the pages before him*.) So, you guys didn't do anything to the A scene?

BELINDA. Oh—

ED. The lawn mower run doesn't work, does it? I mean, it's a good area, it's just not real enough ...

REN. Yeah. I had some ideas but ...

ED. Well, you want to do this now? I mean, we're still working, right?

REN. (*Enthusiastic*.) Yeah! Great ...

BELINDA. Great!

ED. Great.

(*LIGHTS change*.)

Scene 12

Clara and Belinda: CLARA AND BELINDA GET DRUNK

CLARA and BELINDA are in a bar.

CLARA. ... So I go over to Bill's house, right, he's the fucking director what am I supposed to say? Besides, why the hell not, he makes the whole thing sound like an afternoon around the pool with his wife and kids, fun, I could stand to go swimming, this city is so hot and disgusting. So I get there and it turns out that Marguerite and the kids have gone to Jackson Hole for the week. Okay. I'm cool, I'm acting like no big deal, it's still a swimming pool, I'll stay for an hour or something and at least get wet. So he's sitting here and I'm swimming, and I get out of the pool and he's acting like my dad or something, smiling like—it's just creepy, he keeps talking about what a great group we have on the show, it's such a family, do I want something to drink? Do I want to try out the Jacuzzi? And I'm like, no, Bill, I just want to get some sun. And he gets kind of jolly and paternal, and he says, come over here. Let me give you a hug. I'm like, excuse me? I'm in my bathing suit, I'm all wet, he's in his bathing suit, and he wants to give me a *hug*. And he's just sitting there smiling and holding his arms out like Buddha or something—

BELINDA. Oh, gross—

CLARA. And he just keeps sitting there, you know? He doesn't move. So to give him a hug, you have to sit on his lap.

BELINDA. No. Come on.

CLARA. It was completely creepy.

BELINDA. So, did you do it? Did you sit on his lap?

(CLARA looks at her, then away.)

BELINDA. Oh, fuck. This town is amazing. It's like they've institutionalized sexual harassment.

CLARA. Welcome to Hollywood.

BELINDA. They're so blunt about it out here. I mean, at least in academia the harassment was—*subtle*.

CLARA. And it doesn't get you anywhere, either. I mean, the whole point of putting up with harassment is that you get something out of it, right? Explain that to Bill. He had my spec for three weeks. That's why I went over there. Guess what? He still hasn't read it. Next time he asks me to sit on his lap, I'm going to tell him to fuck off and die.

BELINDA. You should've told him the first time.

CLARA. Look, don't give me that shit, I'm just doing the best I—

BELINDA. No, I'm sorry, I didn't—fuck, I know, it's—

CLARA. I shouldn't care, you know? I shouldn't even be out here. This town is bad. The first week I'm here, I'm walking around these gorgeous neighborhoods, Santa Monica, Beverly Hills, thinking, where the fuck are the black people? I drove through Compton just for the fuck of it, and that scared me so bad I went back to Beverly Hills. I called my dad in Dallas, he pulled some strings and got me a job on the lot, so then I'm walking around this major fucking studio, thinking, oh man, I work in the big house now. Fucking Bill says sit on my lap, I almost said, Yassir, Massa. You walk around the lot, maybe catch a glimpse of Whoopi or Denzel off in the distance, they're like fucking gods, you know, we aren't even on the same planet. And everybody keeps telling me how lucky I am. All my friends? I get paid three hundred bucks a week to run errands for white people, and I'm a lucky girl because I got a *job* on the fucking *lot*. I saw an angel on a street corner, and I didn't even think twice. Wings and shit. The whole nine yards. I didn't even blink. She said, get out now, girl, the day of judgment is at hand, get the fuck out of LA, and I said, what, are you kidding? I got a job on the lot!

(Pause.)

BELINDA. You saw an angel?

CLARA. Oh fuck, they're everywhere now, you see them all over, what's the big deal? They're in catalogues, for God's sake. Notecards and shit. There was some Broadway play about angels, they're making a mini-series of it over on the other side of the lot. The place is crawling with angels. Six hundred extras with wings; the whole soundstage looks like this huge, stressed out birdbath. I don't know. The whole thing, it'll kill you if you think about it too hard. Oh, who cares, right? Some of them are real. They have to be. Don't they?

BELINDA. I guess. Yeah, sure.

(CLARA drinks, depressed. BELINDA looks at her.)

BELINDA. You wrote a spec?

CLARA. Every PA on the lot has written a spec.

BELINDA. Well, I'll read it for you.

CLARA. Oh, that'll do me a lot of good. No offense.

BELINDA. No, come on, I know a lot about writing. I used to teach writing. And contrary to what those guys may think, writing is not a competitive sport. You should let me look at it.

CLARA. Okay. Thanks. (*Pause.*) You're not going to last out here, you know.

BELINDA. What?

CLARA. I mean, what the fuck are you doing, having drinks with one of the PA's? What is the matter with you? Don't you have a brain in your head?

BELINDA. What?

CLARA. You're not going to last.

(*THEY stare at each other. LIGHTS change.*)

Scene 13

Steve: WHAT IS COMEDY?

The writers' room. EVERYONE is screaming at each other. Once again, ED is not there.

BELINDA. The scene dies; the whole thing just grinds to a halt—

STEVE. It's just the joke, if we come up with a better—

BELINDA. It's not the joke, it's the scene. We've been waiting for fifteen minutes to find out if she got the job, oh, suspense is building, did she get it, did she—

REN. Maybe there's something in the perfume area, there's got to be a joke in—

BILL. Perfume, that's funny.

SALLY. Perfume that smells like cheese, maybe?

REN. That's funny.

SALLY. 'Cause it's the cheese state, right—

BELINDA. Wisconsin is the cheese state.

STEVE. They're right next to each other. We can fudge it.

REN. Perfume that smells like fudge.

SALLY. For chocolate lovers.

(THEY laugh.)

SALLY. Oh, this is a terrific area, Ren. You are so funny.

BELINDA. Look, all I'm saying is, we're waiting for this information, so if it comes out at the beginning of the scene, there's nothing driving the rest of it.

STEVE. Wait, wait wait. Everyone who smells the stuff hates it, right? Perfume that smells like chocolate. Who would buy this shit? Then a huge fat man comes up to the counter—

REN. Oh, that's perfect—

(EVERYONE except BELINDA is laughing.)

STEVE. He's like, in a trance—

BILL. And Sissy's put the perfume on, right? She's been trying it on, while she talks about dating again—

STEVE. And the fat guy waddles over—

BELINDA. Oh, come on, you guys, not fat jokes; aren't we above anything?

STEVE. Not if it's funny.

BELINDA. Yeah, but come on, this isn't that funny, and besides, Ed keeps talking about the show being *real,* and there's nothing real about a fat man and chocolate perfume. Come on, you guys. We could make this really good. I mean, they're going to put it on television, television is where people now, in our culture, go to hear stories about our lives, and stories are what keep us human. There are so many stories to tell, some days I feel like I'm just *choking* on stories, and if we're not ... I don't know—*diligent*—if it's just *shit,* then, what—(*SHE notices that THEY are all staring at her.*) I'm sorry. I just think that, you know, twenty-five million people are going to watch this, and it really does bother me that we're always turning Sissy into such a moron. We don't have to. The problem here is just a little more structural, and if we figured out a way to—

STEVE. Oh yeah, structure always makes me laugh. Those hilarious structures they teach you in graduate school always lay me flat.

(THEY all laugh.)

BELINDA. That was mean.

STEVE. What?

BELINDA. That was a mean thing to say. The joke is mean, and you are being mean. Now. Here. You're being mean to me.

SALLY. Oh, dear. Did you get up on the wrong side of the bed, Belinda?

BELINDA. No. I did not get up on the wrong side of the bed. I can't remember what side of the bed I got up on; it was so long ago. Look, I'm sorry, I just—this isn't funny. It's just mean.

BILL. Oh, brother.

STEVE. Well, comedy is mean. If you can't take it, then—

BELINDA. No, I can take it. I guess I just never understood it. Comedy is mean. Wow. See, I always thought comedy was wit, and surprise, and insight. But I guess if you can't come up with that stuff, mean will do just as well. Oh. Was that a mean thing to say? Gosh, you should write it down; maybe we could use it in the scene.

(REN snickers. SALLY looks at him; HE lets the smile drop and doodles. SALLY picks up the pencil.)

SALLY. All right, where were we? Perfume counter ...

BELINDA. Fine. Go ahead and write that damn joke. It will never make it in. Ed is going to hate it.

STEVE. Look—

BILL. No, she's right. Ed is going to hate it.

SALLY. I think it's funny.

BELINDA. Well, let's just ask him. Let's call over to editing and ask him. That way we don't waste any more time; it's after midnight already—

SALLY. I think it's funny.

REN. Yeah, me too.

BILL. Oh, yeah, it's hilarious. But I think she's right. It's really not Ed's kind of joke.

(Pause. There is a moment of tense silence.)

REN. So, what else can we use there, there's got to be something else we can put in there.

(Pause. THEY think.)

ED. *(Enters.)* Hey, how's it going, you hacks? Anybody crack this thing yet?

REN. Ed!

SALLY. Ed, hi—

BILL. You finish the cut?

ED. *(Shaking his head.)* It's not coming together. Jim's a fucking mess. Maybe if you took a look at it. *(Off script.)* Whoa. You're still in the D scene?

SALLY. Well. We've been kicking around a few— We were talking about maybe finding a joke in the perfume area.

ED. Perfume jokes? Yikes.

SALLY. No. We had some really funny ideas.

BELINDA. I just think the problem is—

ED. I don't want to know what the problem is, I want to know what the solution is! Jesus, fucking perfume jokes. Do I have to do everything myself?

(HE exits. ALL are left in a tense silence. LIGHTS change.)

Scene 14

Clara: IS THERE COFFEE?

Morning. The writers' room. CLARA is cleaning up. BELINDA enters, frazzled. SHE carries a rough draft manuscript.

CLARA. Hey. How's it going?

BELINDA. I don't know. Ed called me on Friday and said he needed my episode first thing Monday, so I spent the whole weekend writing. How was the weather?

CLARA. Gorgeous.

BELINDA. What a surprise. Can you type this?

CLARA. Sure. I can't wait to meet Benny.

BELINDA. (*Not quite hearing her.*) What?

CLARA. Benny. Sissy's ex-husband.

BELINDA. What about him?

CLARA. Your episode's about Benny, isn't it?

(BELINDA stares at her.)

CLARA. Ed had a meeting with the network last week. They were about to cancel us, so he told them about all the great scripts coming up, and he said you were writing this hilarious episode about Benny. He's been telling everybody.

BELINDA. What?

CLARA. That's why he needed the script this morning. They're casting Bennys this afternoon.

(BILL enters.)

BILL. Hey, how's it going? How's our little machine? I can't wait to meet Benny. Clara, is there coffee?

CLARA. Do you have eyes? Look at the coffee pot. Look at it.

BILL. I love this girl.

BELINDA. Bill, I didn't know anything about Benny.

BILL. Benny, Sissy's ex-husband. It's such a hilarious idea, bringing him on. I can't wait to see what you did with him.

BELINDA. I didn't do anything with him.

BILL. Ed said he called you on Friday—

BELINDA. He did call me on Friday, but he didn't tell me anything about Benny! I thought Benny was an off-stage character, we've been talking for months about how we were never going to see Benny—

BILL. The network wanted Benny. We're casting Benny this afternoon.

BELINDA. There's no Benny.

BILL. You didn't write anything for Benny? Oh, Jesus. What the fuck are we supposed to use for sides?

STEVE. *(Enters.)* Hey, how's it going? So, today's the big day we meet Benny. Clara, is there coffee?

CLARA. Why are people always asking me that?

BILL. *(To Steve.)* She forgot Benny.

STEVE. She *what*?

BELINDA. *(Overlap.)* I didn't forget Benny, no one told me!

STEVE. Aren't we casting Benny this afternoon?

BILL. Except we have no sides.

CLARA. You want me to type this, the way it is?
BILL. No.
BELINDA. It's all I've got—
STEVE. You forgot *Benny*? Whoa.
BELINDA.I didn't forget him.
BILL. Ed's gonna have a fit.
ED. (*Enters.*) Hey, how's it going? Can't wait to meet Benny. Clara, is there coffee?
CLARA. I can't believe how difficult this coffee thing is for everybody. No one can tell if it's here. No one can pour their own cup ...
ED. I love this girl.
BELINDA. Ed, you didn't tell me about Benny.

(ED turns and looks at her. SHE forges ahead.)

BELINDA. I just spent the whole weekend working on my script, because you said you needed it today, but you didn't say anything about Benny. And I can do it, if you want me to invent this guy Benny, that's fine, I can do that, I can write a whole episode about Benny, I can do anything with Benny that you want, but you have to tell me. You told everybody else. Why didn't you tell me?
ED. (*Stares at her.*) Look, you've got an hour. It's no big deal. Just introduce Benny. Write a little scene for him. Maybe something on a stoop in the rain on a college campus. It can be a flashback, we'll give everybody funny hair. I wrote a scene like that for my movie and it never got in. It was hilarious.
STEVE. I remember that scene. It was.
ED. So, you guys up for some hoops this afternoon?
BILL. Isn't it supposed to get pretty hot today?

STEVE. I heard it was gonna be in the nineties.
ED. Wimps.

(THEY go. CLARA watches BELINDA, who sits at the table.)

CLARA. You still want me to type that?
BELINDA. This episode's not about Benny. Benny belongs in it about as much as the fucking tooth fairy. I'm going to have to rewrite it from scratch, I just spent the weekend working on an episode that's completely USELESS, I was up till four last night, I haven't had a day off in MONTHS and he's acting like I'm the one who's nuts. WHAT THE FUCK IS THE MATTER WITH THESE PEOPLE?
CLARA. Belinda ... Don't let them get in.
BELINDA. What?
CLARA. You want some coffee? Let me get you some coffee. Here. Have some coffee. *(SHE pours Belinda coffee.)*

(LIGHTS change.)

Scene 15

Belinda: AFTER TWO

BELINDA sits in the writers' room. SHE smokes. After a moment, REN enters.

REN. Belinda?

BELINDA. Oh, Jesus. You scared me.

REN. What are you doing here? Everything's done, isn't it?

BELINDA. Yeah, I was just having a cigarette. I probably shouldn't be smoking in here. You know Sally's just going to throw a fit. Don't tell her I said that.

REN. Are you okay?

BELINDA. Yeah, sure.

(SHE smokes. HE watches her.)

REN. You going over to the garage?

BELINDA. No, you go ahead. I'll be out of here in a minute.

REN. I don't mind waiting.

BELINDA. Look, I'm fine, all right?

REN. It's after two.

BELINDA. Yeah, so maybe we'll get lucky; maybe some nice little psychopath will find me alone and come after me with a hatchet. It'd be a real break for you, Ren; once I'm out of here they're going to make you a producer like that.

(SHE snaps her fingers. HE looks at her.)

BELINDA. Sorry.

(Clearly, SHE's not. After a moment, REN crosses, takes a cigarette and lights it. HE sits. SHE watches him.)

REN. So, what's up with you?

BELINDA. Nothing's up. I'm just a little depressed.

REN. How come?

BELINDA. Gee, I don't know. I just moved three thousand miles to the ugliest city in America, I work eighty hours a week, I don't get any sleep, my writing is for shit and everybody hates me. I don't know why I'm depressed. If you can't be happy here, you can't be happy anywhere. Right?

REN. What are you talking about? Nobody hates you. They all love you here.

BELINDA. Secretly, they hate me. Maybe I'm not depressed. Maybe I'm paranoid.

REN. Maybe you are.

BELINDA. (*Snapping.*) Yeah, what would you know about it, Golden Boy?

REN. Belinda—

BELINDA. I'm sorry. I'm a little tense. I started therapy this week; I think it's making me—

REN. Really? You're in therapy?

BELINDA. Yeah, so what, you've never been in therapy? *Everyone* does therapy—

REN. Feeling a little defensive about it?

BELINDA. (*Beat.*) Maybe. Defensive, depressed and paranoid. Good thing I'm in therapy.

(*Pause.*)

REN. What made you go?

BELINDA. (*Matter of fact, almost good humored.*) I couldn't get off the floor. Saturday morning. I got up and took a shower, and then I went back to my bedroom, and I was looking for this shirt, in a pile of clothes on the floor, and I just ... put my head down and started crying, and I

couldn't get up. I couldn't get off the floor, for like ...
three hours. (*Pause.*) Pretty weird, huh?

REN. Jesus, Belinda. Why didn't you call me?

BELINDA. What?

REN. You should've called me. I could've come over
and made you lunch or something. We could've gone to a
movie. Something.

BELINDA. It's okay. I improvised and went into
therapy instead.

REN. What is it, are you lonely?

BELINDA. (*Pause.*) Look, I'm fine—

REN. Do you want to go have a drink?

BELINDA. Oh, no, come on—

REN. What, you're just sitting here anyway—

BELINDA. I don't need you feeling sorry for me.

REN. Yes, you do. You need someone to feel sorry for
you and then be really, really nice to you for a whole hour
or something. Come on, we'll go to an all-night
supermarket, buy a bottle of champagne and drink it in the
parking lot.

(*HE takes her by the hand and pulls her up. SHE leans her
head against his shoulder for a second.*)

REN. Come on, you're okay.

BELINDA. I know! It's just—nothing. Thanks.

(*THEY look at each other. After a moment, HE leans in
slowly and kisses her. After a moment of uncertainty,
SHE kisses him back. SHE pushes him away. THEY*

look at each other. After a moment, THEY kiss again.
The kiss quickly becomes passionate and THEY wind
up on the table.)

BLACKOUT

END ACT I

ACT II

Scene 1

Clara: THE ANGEL IN LOS ANGELES

*CLARA wears wings and sunglasses and speaks to the
audience.*

CLARA. This is the way the universe works:
Everything moves from imagination to reality. Such is the
force of creation. As soon as anyone imagines anything, it
is only instants away from becoming real. Magic is the
power that makes this happen. Science also has power, but
in a smaller way. You think of objects—a telephone, a
refrigerator, an airplane, and then, they exist. From the
imagination, to the real.

In America, somehow this process has been reversed.
Americans look at something that is only imaginary, and
then transform the real into that imagined thing. Little
girls look at billboards of impossible women and say, that
is what I want to be. People watch moving images of
beings who could never exist, and say, that is what we are.
The real yearns to be imaginary. And so, America is
evaporating. This problem is particularly acute in Los
Angeles, a city which is, frankly, about to lift off. Maybe
that is why they call it the City of the Angels. Although
that too is something of a misnomer. Really, we don't like
it here.

(LIGHTS change.)

Scene 2

Ren: THE ROOKIE PHENOM

REN and BELINDA are in bed in his apartment. HE is reading a script. SHE is going through catalogues.

BELINDA. You hear the one about the megalomaniac baseball team?

REN. No.

BELINDA. Norman Lear has first base, Jim Brooks has second, Cosby third, and Ed has the whole outfield.

(REN smiles, scribbling.)

REN. Come on, he's not that bad.

BELINDA. You know what he told me about that stupid movie he made, I saw that thing, it's the worst movie ever, right? Am I right?

REN. It's not *Citizen Kane*. Okay. It's the worst movie ever.

BELINDA. Exactly. He told me, it was his autobiography. The thing is an adaptation of somebody else's *book,* this other guy wrote the book, and Ed is running around telling everybody it's his autobiography.

REN. He was being metaphoric.

BELINDA. Ed is incapable of being metaphoric. I mean, with all due respect, the guy's a fruitcake, and you're just defending him because he's decided you're his "son." The fact that you grew up in somebody else's house notwithstanding.

REN. Hey. If Ed's decided I'm his son, who am I to say I'm not?

BELINDA. Oh, it's all bullshit anyway. And if I hear one more word about how decent it all is, I may truly puke.

REN. What is the matter with you all of a sudden? What happened to television being like a campfire and you're the great storyteller?

BELINDA. Oh, come on—

REN. No, you come on. You watch a rerun of *The Odd Couple* some night. That show was a thing of beauty. Tony Randall's commitment and, and timing and *pathos*—

BELINDA. Pathos?

REN. Yeah, pathos, you don't see that—I mean, I've read Moliere—

BELINDA. Moliere? How did Moliere—

REN. Yeah, big surprise, the dumb jock reads Moliere.

BELINDA. I didn't say—

REN. And frankly, I don't see the difference.

BELINDA. The difference? Between Tony Randall and Moliere?

REN. Yeah, that's right. What's so fucking different, Miss Ph.D. in English? You tell me what's so different.

BELINDA. (*Overlap.*) Could we not bring my Ph.D. into this, I'm not—

REN. Just answer the question.

BELINDA. You want me to tell you the difference between Tony Randall and Moliere.

REN. That's right. Why is fucking Moliere so much better than Tony Randall?

BELINDA. I don't know, he just is.

REN. He just is, that's a real compelling argument—

BELINDA. All right. The sophistication of his language, his profound understanding and compassion for human nature even while he's satirizing social—

REN. He's telling the same stories we are. Who gets the girl. Fathers and sons competing with each other—

BELINDA. Oh, come on, Ren, theatre and television are completely different experiences. The theatre is much more—vivid, it's more *humane*—

REN. Yeah, I have seen some class A shit in the theatre.

BELINDA. Of course, but—

REN. In fact, most of what passes for theatre is class A shit. The only people who write for the theatre these days are people who can't get work in television.

BELINDA. Oh, is that so?

REN. And I've read your fucking *New Yorker*, too. Boy, that's good writing.

BELINDA. Ren!

REN. What?

BELINDA. What's the matter?

REN. Nothing. (*Pause.*) I just, I think there's been some great television, and I'd like to write some. Someday. I mean, we're telling stories, right? You're the one who made me feel like this. When you talk about it, sometimes, you make it sound like something holy.

BELINDA. Well, I'm full of shit.

REN. No, you're not.

BELINDA. Yes, I am! Christ, we spend all this time, as a group, going over and over these damn scripts—who *ever* decided that writing was a group activity, that's what I want to know. And you know what else I want to know? Why, if we're going to do ten drafts of a script, it doesn't get better! Why not just shoot the first bad draft? Why shoot the *tenth*? Why do Steve and Sally get to fuck up my work? Why does Ed? I mean, all of this—it isn't about storytelling. It's not even about product. It's just about power.

REN. Then why are you doing it?

BELINDA. (*Pause.*) For the money. (*Pause.*) I mean, I've never had money. I know, you think it's chicken feed, but this is more money than I've ever *dreamed* of, this is— That's the thing about selling your soul. No one tells you how much they'll actually pay you for it.

REN. You're not selling your soul. I can't believe you. I'd kill to be able to write like you, and all you do is run it down. Never mind.

(HE goes back to the script. SHE watches him, uncertain, a little embarrassed.)

BELINDA. I'm sorry.

REN. You don't have to be sorry. I'm sorry. I'm sorry you don't enjoy this more.

BELINDA. (*Making up.*) I'm starting to enjoy it. I'm starting to enjoy it a lot.

REN. Well, you should. Ed is crazy about you. And you love him. Whether you want to admit it or not.

BELINDA. I never said I didn't like Ed. I think he's a nut, and I'm also desperate for his approval. It's an ongoing topic of discussion between me and my therapist.

REN. Well, stop worrying about it. You know, he's bumping up your next episode. He called me yesterday, raving about it.

BELINDA. (*Pause. Positively glowing.*) He did? He liked my script?

REN. He loved it. He loves you. He loves the way you fight—

BELINDA. Forget Ed. What do you like?

REN. I don't like anything at all.

(THEY kiss.)

REN. Okay. That's all you get.
BELINDA. Come on ...
REN. I'm working!

(Giggling, SHE falls back, watches him for a moment, then looks through her catalogues.)

BELINDA. (*Musing.*) Hey, Ren? What did you do when you first started making money? I mean, was there a moment when all of a sudden, you had money? You didn't have any, and then you just, had a lot?

REN. Yeah, sure.

BELINDA. What did you do?

REN. I don't know, I ... I bought, uh, a box of chocolates. You know, like, a five pound box of See's chocolates, and I ... Fed-Exed it to my grandmother.

BELINDA. You sent your grandma chocolates? That is so—

REN. Yeah, okay—

BELINDA. It's adorable!

REN. So what did you do?

BELINDA. I bought sheets. I realized I've been sleeping on the same sheets since college; they're always so expensive, I could never justify buying new ones. So I bought these pretty sheets, with colors, and ... I'm sorry, I'm embarrassed now. After that spectacular grandma story, I sound so—

REN. No, you don't.

BELINDA. It's just so weird, actually having it. I don't quite know how to spend it.

REN. Tell you what. This weekend, we'll go to San Francisco, rent a suite at the Ritz, and never leave. Order up room service for two days.

BELINDA. Oh, yeah? What will we be doing for two days?

REN. We will be watching basketball on TV.

BELINDA. (*SHE laughs.*) You are so mean.

REN. Basketball is a beautiful thing.

BELINDA. So how come you quit? I mean, you were a big college star, right? Why didn't you keep going?

REN. Because I was awful. I was the worst basketball player, ever.

BELINDA. But you were in all those big games, weren't you?

REN. Yeah, "big games." That's the NC double A to you, babe. I didn't really play in those games. The coach basically kept me on the team because he liked me.

BELINDA. I don't believe you. Ed says you're great.

REN. Compared to Ed, I am. He is old and weak, and I am young and hard.

BELINDA. (*Laughing.*) Ed's no good?

REN. Terrible.

BELINDA. How's Bill?

REN. Sucks.

BELINDA. Wait a minute. If you guys all stink, maybe I could play with you.

REN. No.

BELINDA. (*Baiting him.*) Why not?

REN. (*Beat.*) You're not tall enough.

(*HE kisses her as SHE laughs.*)

BLACKOUT

Scene 3

Belinda: THE FAMILY OF MANN III

The Mann family kitchen. DAVE and WILLY are arguing.

UNCLE WILLY. The situation is not grim, Dave. Not grim at all.

DAVE. The car is a lemon. I took you into my home, put a roof over your head, and you sold my daughter a lemon. Your own niece!

UNCLE WILLY. Now, Dave, you're not looking at this right.

DAVE. I'm looking at a lemon!

UNCLE WILLY. You know, cars are like people, Dave. Each one has a different personality and no one is perfect.

DAVE. Don't start this, Willy. I don't want to have to hurt you.

UNCLE WILLY. But we all try to make ourselves better. Don't we? I know I do. I know I'm always searching for my best self. Well, cars search too.

DAVE. Willy, she's had this car for less than twenty-four hours and the fuel line is leaking, smoke is coming from somewhere ... everywhere ...

UNCLE WILLY. Is there ever a good time for trouble, Dave? For some of us, it comes early, and for some it comes late. But trouble is an important part of life's journey! You would never call a person a lemon, Dave.

DAVE. Oh, I might.

UNCLE WILLY. No, not you. Not my big brother Dave. I loathe you, you big lug.

(SISSY enters, followed by BUDDY, who has soot on his face.)

UNCLE WILLY. Sissy! Aren't you looking like a fresh spring morning.

SISSY. Thank you, Uncle Willy. Uncle Willy, is there something wrong with my new car? It's spouting dust everywhere. Buddy was trying to help—

BUDDY. Anything for you, Sis—

SISSY. But it just keeps blowing up!

UNCLE WILLY. Oh, no, that's perfectly natural for—

DAVE. Sweetheart?

SISSY. Yes, Daddy.

DAVE. You know I love you.

SISSY. Oh, thank you, Daddy.

DAVE. Could vou go back outside for a minute? I'm going to have to hurt Uncle Willy, and I don't want you to have to see it.

SISSY. Oh.

UNCLE WILLY. Sissy—you know, Sissy, what would go beautifully with your hair today? A 1982 Volvo with new whitewalls and a moonroof.

SISSY. (*Sweet.*) Oh, Uncle Willy. You always say the sweetest things. (*Abrupt.*) I'm sorry, do I have—do I have to say this? This is so stupid.

UNCLE WILLY. I don't even have that. What is that?

SISSY. I can't make this work. It's not even funny.

(WILLY looks at her script. BILL enters, flustered.)

BILL. What's the problem? Jesus. What's the problem now? Monica, you're supposed to cross—

BUDDY. What? They cut my—I had a whole speech there.

SISSY. It's bullshit, Bill. Come on, you know it is.

DAVE. (*Overlap.*) I don't have these pages, either. What color is that, salmon? I don't have salmon pages.

BUDDY. Salmon? I didn't get salmon pages.

UNCLE WILLY. I haven't seen any salmon pages.

BILL. Oh, Jesus. Could someone call up to the writers and—(*Yelling out.*) Who the fuck fucked up this time?

SISSY. I mean, *I* can write better than this. Bill!

BILL. Look, Monica, this is not a fight you want to pick. Ed's under a lot of pressure right now, and besides, the writing on this show is excellent; you should see the shit they make you say on other shows. (*Yelling out.*) Could someone take care of this, please? Are we getting new pages?

SISSY. "You always say the sweetest things" is excellent? What am I, a complete moron?

DAVE. Sweetheart, you want Shakespeare, go to New York. You can do it in Central Park; they'll pay you three hundred bucks a week. Here, you make ten thousand a week doing shit. So shut up.

BILL. People. People!

DAVE. And could you get him to say the line right? It's I *love* you, not I *loathe* you. He's doing it on purpose.

BILL. It sounded fine to me, Jim.

UNCLE WILLY. I say the line that's written.

DAVE. He said I *loathe* you!

BUDDY. So where are these salmon pages? I don't have 'em.

CLARA. (*Enters, frantic.*) Here they are! I'm sorry. (*SHE starts to pass out pages.*)

BILL. So what the fuck is going on, Clara? This is, we can't have this. We lost, like, fifteen minutes here trying to figure out if everybody's even in the same scene.

CLARA. I don't know what happened, Bill. I wasn't here this morning when the pages were distributed.

BILL. So who's in charge of this, can you tell me that?

CLARA. I don't know, Bill; I'll find out as soon as I get this—

BILL. (*Snapping.*) Don't you fucking raise your voice to me! (*There is silence on the set.*) I don't need some little shit PA talking back to me. You fucked up. You cost this operation thousands of dollars because you were fucking careless. And now you're going to stand there and tell me this isn't your fault?

CLARA. I think I have a right to defend myself.

BILL. You have no fucking rights, you little shit! What makes you think your job affords you any dignity at all? You're a PA! You're nothing! And you fucked up. Do you understand? Do you understand anything at all? You're shit. You are nothing but shit here. No one wants to hear what you did wrong. Get out of here. (*Pause.*) Get out!

(SHE goes. HE turns back to the actors.)

BILL. Okay, the show's over. Could we do some work here? (*HE sits.*)

(LIGHTS change.)

Scene 4

Buddy: WE COULD HELP

STEVE is sitting in the writers' room. BELINDA enters.

BELINDA. Oh, hi. Where is everybody?
STEVE. I don't know. I thought we were meeting.
BELINDA. Well, yeah, I thought so, too. Clara?

(CLARA enters.)

BELINDA. Do you know where everybody is?

CLARA. Bill's on the set, Ren and Ed are editing, and Sally's at wardrobe.

BELINDA. I thought we were meeting.

CLARA. Ed postponed till after lunch.

BELINDA. Oh, okay. Great.

(CLARA exits. BELINDA starts to go.)

STEVE. As long as we've got time, we could go over your script.

BELINDA. Oh. By ourselves?

STEVE. Well, I took a pass at it last night. I mean, it's good. I just had some ideas about the second act. To pop the comedy a little.

BELINDA. Oh. Well, shouldn't we wait until the whole group is together so that we don't ... repeat?

STEVE. Are you doing something else right now? I just want to help. This is your first show, and I've done this a lot, and I consider it my responsibility to—help. Is that a problem?

BELINDA. No! No, of course not, I—

BILL. *(Enters.)* Is Ed in here? Where is everybody?

BELINDA. Ed's in editing with Ren, Sally's in wardrobe.

BILL. Great. Jim just had a major meltdown.

STEVE. What happened?

BILL. Apparently, Monica was on the *Today* show this morning, so he's livid. Some asshole reporter said, on the air, that she's the real star of the show. So now nothing's right. Jim's costume's fucked, the scene's fucked, I'm fucked—

STEVE. Oh, Jesus.

BELINDA. You want me to go get Ed?

BILL. Please. He's not going down to the set for this kind of shit. What are we doing for lunch?

BELINDA. I don't know. I was gonna grab Ren. I'll tell Ed you're looking for him.

BILL. Oh, you're going over there?

BELINDA. Yeah, Ren and I are supposed to have lunch.

REN. (*Enters.*) Hey, you ready?

BELINDA. Oh, you're here.

REN. Ed had to go do an interview.

BILL. Where are you going? Commissary?

BELINDA. Actually, I think we were going to go off the lot for a change. You want to come?

BILL. No. You go ahead.

(THEY go. BILL shakes his head.)

BILL. Can you fucking believe it?

STEVE. What?

BILL. Ren and Belinda. They're sleeping together. Man, it didn't take them long.

STEVE. You're kidding.

BILL. You couldn't tell? Shit. I just hope Ed doesn't find out. He hates that shit. And Sally's going to have heart failure.

STEVE. Sally? Why should she care?

BILL. Jesus, Steve. Where are you?

SALLY. (*Enters.*) I'm sorry I'm late. Oh, aren't we meeting?

STEVE. Ed postponed till after lunch.

SALLY. Oh, God. I hate it when he does this. We're falling behind already and it's much too early in the season. We don't even have our pickup yet, and he's already—

BILL. We're fine. Belinda's new script just came in; it's terrific. Did you read it?

SALLY. Of course I read it. I think it needs work.

BILL. What, are you kidding? It's great. It reads like a fucking *Cheers* episode. If we've got an Emmy script, that's the one. Well, I'll go see if Jim's calmed down. He's going to be hell until we get the pickup.

(HE goes. SALLY and STEVE sit in silence for a moment.)

SALLY. What is he talking about? That script needs a lot of help.

STEVE. I agree.

SALLY. I can't believe this. I mean, where is she? We could be working on it, even if Ed's not here. We could take an initial pass.

STEVE. She's having lunch with Ren.

SALLY. You're kidding. It's eleven thirty in the morning. What are they going to lunch now for?

STEVE. Apparently, they're sleeping together.

(THEY look at each other.
LIGHTS change.)

Scene 5

Sally: SHE'S GREAT

ED is in his office. SALLY enters.

ED. Hey, what's up?

SALLY. Nothing major. I just have some Polaroids for you to look at. Jim keeps changing his mind about what he's wearing this week. He wants you to look at it.

(SHE hands him the Polaroids.)

ED. Oh, Jesus. Like I got nothing better to do.

SALLY. I told him, but he's gone completely insane. Ever since Monica did the *Today* show, he's been impossible.

ED. He's just uptight about the numbers. Everybody's got a lot riding on this. Here, this one.

SALLY. Great, that's the one everybody likes. So, are we going to take a pass at Belinda's script before it goes to table?

ED. Well, there's not a lot to do on it. I thought she and Ren and I would just take a look at it tonight, see if we can punch anything up.

SALLY. Oh. Sure. You don't want Steve and I to stick around, then?

ED. Yeah, you know, you guys, we should get you going on another couple of scripts, so if you could put some things together, ideas, that's probably the best use of your time.

SALLY. Sure. That sounds great. (*Pause.*) Belinda's script really is terrific. Everyone's saying it could be our Emmy.

ED. Really?

SALLY. That's what Bill was saying. The crew is wild for it.

ED. Well, Jesus. I don't know about any Emmys. She's a kid. It's her third script.

SALLY. Oh, I know. That's just what people are saying. I mean, she and Ren are just great. You know, Ren's good, and she's really good.

ED. They're both good.

SALLY. But she's special, she really is. Everyone's noticed it.

ED. Yeah. I was the first to notice it, remember? I hired her.

SALLY. Oh, I know. She's really a find. Oh, one other thing. I was talking to some reporter this morning, from *Redbook* or something, who went off on this kick about not knowing how Dave fit into the show. Now—I tried to get her off this, because that idiot on the *Today* show said exactly the same thing to Monica.

ED. Oh, Jesus. Jim's going to throw a fit.

SALLY. That's what I thought. Anyway, I'm just not sure I convinced her, and the next thing you know, we're going to be in one of those situations where everyone's saying the star isn't the star—

ED. Yeah, yeah, yeah—

SALLY. Do you want to give her a call?

ED. Yeah, sure.

SALLY. I'll have Clara send the number over.

BELINDA. (*Enters.*) Hey, what's going on?

SALLY. What do you mean?

BELINDA. (*Pause.*) Well—Ren and I are over in the writers' building. Where is everybody? Aren't we starting the rewrite soon?

SALLY. Steve and I are taking the night off.

BELINDA. You are?

ED. Yeah, I thought the three of us could handle it. There's not a lot. Mostly we just need to take a pass and see if we can't make Dave more central to the episode.

BELINDA. (*Slight pause.*) What?

ED. Yeah, I just think, you know, we gotta keep our focus on our guy. Keep him central. He's the person everyone's coming to see. I just don't think this script really answers the question Why is this important to Dave? just yet.

BELINDA. Well—

ED. (*A little dangerous.*) You have a problem?

BELINDA. No! I just, you know, it's—this episode's not really *about* Dave. Off the top of my head, I just don't see how we're going to graft him in.

(*ED stares at her. There is an uncomfortable pause.*)

SALLY. Have a fun rewrite! (*SHE goes.*)

(*LIGHTS change.*)

Scene 6

THE FAMILY OF MANN IV

The LIGHTS come low up on ED, in his office.

ED. (*Quiet.*) I don't feel good. I don't *feel* good. You think I don't know what's going on? You think I'm stupid? I know what they want. Fighting amongst themselves. Trying to destroy each other. When I'm the one they're really after. You think I don't know that? You think I can't see it in their eyes? They're cannibals! They'd eat me alive if they could. That's what happened to the gods, you know. Their children ate them. For their strength. Why should I be any different? Well, fuck them. Fuck them all. Not one of them could handle this. Not ONE. The networks. The fucking numbers. Reporters. The assholes who advertise on this fucking show. FUCKING ACTORS. Every fucking day I deal with shit, with FUCKING SHIT, I keep everyone from destroying those fuckers, I spend my life providing for all of them, and they TURN on me. You think I don't *KNOW*?

GINNY. Dave? Are you all right, sweetheart? Why are you sitting in the dark?

DAVE. What, darling?

GINNY. Oh, you poor darling. You're upset about something!

DAVE. Oh, no.

GINNY. But you are, sweetheart. Your little forehead is getting all bunched up. Oh. Let me take care of you. Let me make you a cup of tea. Buddy! Sissy! Come down here and take care of your father! He's upset.

DAVE. That's okay, Ginny. Let the kids sleep.

GINNY. No, I want them down here, Dave, so you can see what a fortunate man you are. Your whole family is with you. Your kids, your brother. A lot of people might think, what a lot of good-for-nothing freeloaders. But you're glad they're here!

DAVE. I guess I am.

GINNY. I must admit, I sometimes worry. Maybe it would be better for Willy and the kids if they went out and lived their own lives. But it wouldn't be better for *you*.

DAVE. You think so, honey?

GINNY. I know it. You like it like this. Everyone here, under your control.

DAVE. Under my power.

GINNY. It makes you feel great.

DAVE. That's true.

GINNY. And that's why we stay. To make you happy. That's the only reason. Kids! Where are you? Your father needs you!

DAVE. Is that true, Ginny? You're all here, for me?

GINNY. Of course it is, sweetheart!

(BUDDY and SISSY enter.)

BUDDY. Hey! What's everyone doing up?

GINNY. We were just talking about how glad we are to have you kids back home with us. You see, most people don't understand how perfect our world is.

DAVE. What could be better? I'm the king, and everyone else serves my needs. In return, I protect you and give you things. Money. Presents.

BUDDY. We earn some of that stuff, Dad. Yesterday, I did mow the lawn.

DAVE. Yes, you did, son. Not as well as I would have. But what the hey.

SISSY. Oh, Daddy. I love you so much. Would you like some more tea?

DAVE. That would be great, honey.

GINNY. I'm just going to go stand off in the corner here, Dave. I know how much you prefer the company of these young, healthy kids. If you need anything, just give a holler.

DAVE. Thanks, Ginny. You're so understanding.

UNCLE WILLY. Hey! What about me?

BUDDY and SISSY. Uncle Willy!

DAVE. Come on over here, Willy, you old coot, and let me shove my fist up your ass!

(DAVE and WILLY laugh heartily.)

REN. Hey, are you two having good manly fun over over there? I want to get in on this! How about I shove my fist up your ass!

(THEY laugh.)

UNCLE WILLY. And then I'll shove my fist up your ass!

REN. And then I'll shove my fist up your ass!

(THEY laugh.)

DAVE. And then we can all play basketball! And you girls can cheer us on!

SISSY. (*Dry.*) Yeah, that sounds like fun.

(*The MEN all stop laughing. THEY stare at her.*)

SISSY. (*With forced enthusiasm.*) I mean, that sounds like *fun*! That sounds like fun!

(*THEY continue to stare at her.*)

BELINDA. I'm trying, all right? And how much longer am I going to have to hold this fucking teapot?
GINNY. Sissy!
BELINDA. Oh, come on, he's not actually buying this shit, is he? I mean, do you really need me here? Can't I just go read a book?
DAVE. Sissy, are you feeling left out?
BELINDA. Left out? No. Pissed off is closer to what I'm running into here. I mean, this is so boring. Do any of you know people who are like this? And would you want to? Why are we doing this?
DAVE. (*Beat.*) You're not Sissy. You're not my daughter at all. Where's Sissy?
BELINDA. I ate her. (*SHE laughs maniacally.*)
DAVE. Sissy? Sissy! SISSSSYYYY!

(*As DAVE howls and BELINDA laughs, the OTHERS turn and scatter.*)

BLACKOUT

Scene 7

Clara: ED WANTS TO SEE YOU

BELINDA stands at the door of Ed's office.

BELINDA. You wanted to see me?
ED. Yeah, come on in. Have a seat.

(SHE does. ED looks up and speaks easily but abruptly.)

ED. I've been thinking about this, and I don't think you'll ever be happy here, and I think you should leave the show. It's up to you, but that's what I think.

(Pause.)

BELINDA. (*In shock.*) Okay.

(ED looks at her, stunned and outraged.)

ED. All right. Fine. (*Pause.*) That's all.

(HE gestures to the door. SHE stands and looks at him, confused.)

BELINDA. Wait a minute. Is this really what you want? You want me to leave the show. That's what you want?
ED. I think … you are never going to be happy here, and … it's up to you, but I think you should leave.

BELINDA. Yesterday you told me I was talented, and valuable and—now you want me to leave? I don't understand.

ED. It's your decision.

BELINDA. For heaven's sake, Ed, you're the executive producer. If you want me to leave, it's not my decision!

ED. It's interesting to hear you say that. You didn't seem to feel that way yesterday.

BELINDA. Yesterday, what? You mean last night? What did I say? I said, I thought that grafting Dave into the episode might not—

ED. I don't graft. I DON'T GRAFT. And if you're not willing to rewrite, then—

BELINDA. You wanted to rewrite an episode that worked!

ED. I decide what works!

BELINDA. Two days ago, you loved that episode. Everyone loves that episode—

ED. (*Overlap.*) And if one day I say it works and the next day I say it's shit, then that's the way it is. You clearly don't understand the process. When I was working on my movie, I would go home every night and rewrite scenes for the next day!

BELINDA. But I was willing to stay! I didn't think it was necessary, but I would have done it—

ED. You didn't think it was necessary? You're making these decisions now?

BELINDA. You were the one who called off the rewrite. You said we'd do it today! Ed, listen. I am not trying to contradict you. I have nothing but admiration for your movie ... and your ... brilliance. But yesterday, I listened to you with that reporter on the phone, and I thought, you seemed to be panicking. I just thought it was my job to reassure you that the episode was good, and you didn't have to panic.

ED. I don't need some little girl telling me what's good and what's not.

BELINDA. (*Flaring again.*) Look, if you're going to stick fruit loops in one of my episodes because someone crossed their eyes at you over lunch, I think I have a right to at least—

ED. Your episode? Your episode? Let me tell you something. There isn't any episode that's *yours*. There is only *my* show. *I* write this show. Don't you ever talk about your episodes again.

BELINDA. Oh, Jesus, everybody talks about their episodes, we always—Ren practically blew a gasket last week because you bumped his episode in the release order and you didn't ask him to leave!

ED. That was a different situation. I was in a different mood then.

BELINDA. So I'm being fired because you're having a bad day?

ED. It's up to you.

(*Pause.*)

BELINDA. I'll have my agent give you a call.

(*SHE goes. ED's head twitches for a moment, then HE sits. CLARA enters, carrying a script.*)

CLARA. Hey, Ed, you wanted to look at proofs for next week? (*Pause.*) Ed?

ED. Belinda's out of here. She's out.

*(CLARA stares at him, stunned.
LIGHTS change.)*

Scene 8

Ren: BELINDA BLOWS A GASKET

*Ren's office. BELINDA paces, furious and frantic. REN
sits, confused.*

BELINDA. Then, THEN he gives me the line about
that fucking movie, when he was working on his MOVIE,
he went home every night and rewrote scenes for the next
day. I'm thinking, oh, and what a blinding achievement
that piece of shit was, Ed.

REN. Belinda, you have to keep it down; the
secretaries—

BELINDA. I don't give a *shit* who hears. That fucking
piece of shit fired me over nothing; he's screaming at me
that no little girl is going to tell him anything; can you
FUCKING believe that prick called me a little GIRL—

REN. BELINDA. You have to be quiet now. You just,
you have to be quiet.

BELINDA. I'm sorry. I'm sorry.

(SHE starts to cry. HE crosses and holds her.)

BELINDA. I just don't—what happened? I mean, you hear about this shit going on, but who the fuck knew it actually did?

BILL. (*Enters.*) What's going on? We can hear you guys yelling in here all over the building, what's—

BELINDA. Ed asked me to leave the show.

BILL. What? Oh, fuck. Oh, Jesus.

BELINDA. That fucking *prick*—

REN. Belinda.

BILL. He didn't mean it.

BELINDA. He was very specific, Bill—

BILL. What did he say?

BELINDA. He said he thought I should leave the show! But it's up to me. Is that the most passive aggressive bullshit you've ever—

REN. *Belinda.*

BILL. No, he means it. I mean, he means you don't have to go. You have to go back in there and apologize.

BELINDA. What? What am I apologizing for?

BILL. Look, you're upset, you're crying, just go back and tell him you're sorry, it's all he wanted. He doesn't want you to leave.

BELINDA. I'm not going to cry for him.

REN. You're crying now. (*SHE stares at him.*) What? If you can cry for us, you can cry for him, what's the difference?

BILL. Look. Ed is under a lot of pressure, his wife is bugging him to get out of television, the show isn't getting the numbers he wanted, he wants to get rid of Steve and Sally, but he can't—

BELINDA. So he got rid of me instead?

BILL. No, he doesn't want to get rid of you. That's not what he wanted. He just wants your loyalty. He needs you to say, I'm here for you, Ed.

BELINDA. While he's telling me to leave?

BILL. He didn't say that. He said it was up to you. You cannot leave him.

BELINDA. He told me to leave!

BILL. That's not what he told you.

REN. Look, what did he say? What did you do to piss him off?

BELINDA. I didn't—I don't know, it was—

BILL. Look, you can't fall apart on us, Belinda. The show needs you. There can be no ego involved here!

BELINDA. What do you mean, no ego, I don't even know what that—

BILL. You do not exist. Do you understand me? The only person who exists here is Ed. He is the executive producer. It is his show, his vision, and you do whatever he wants.

BELINDA. He wants me to leave the show!

REN. He said it was up to you.

BELINDA. Oh, man. Don't you both fucking gang up on me—

BILL. You cannot leave him. No writer has ever left Ed and gone on to work on anything of significance. Anywhere.

BELINDA. What?

BILL. All I'm saying is no writer has ever left Ed and gone on to work on anything of any significance.

BELINDA. What are you saying, I only exist in relation to Ed? If I leave, I cease to exist, I'm no longer a writer, is that what you're fucking telling me?

BILL. This is not about ego, Belinda!

BELINDA. I mean, I love this! He fires me on a whim, and now you're telling me that if I don't get down on my knees and beg for my job back, I'm being egotistical!

REN. Okay, okay, I'm taking you home—

BELINDA. Don't you touch me!

REN. Belinda, Jesus, would you stop, would you just—

BILL. She cannot leave the lot. I'm telling you, I've seen this happen before; she has to go back now, before he gets used to the idea and can't even—

REN. I'm just saying if we send her in there now, while she's still acting like a raving lunatic, it's not going to—

BELINDA. Well, thank you very much and could you all not talk about me as if I'm not even in the room? Jesus, you guys are starting to sound like Ed.

BILL. Belinda, Ed is a genius.

BELINDA. He's not a genius, he's a TV producer! (*Pause.*) And, a megalomaniac. And a madman. And what's more, everybody knows it. (*SHE goes.*)

REN. Oh, Christ.

BILL. That's it. It's over.

REN. Come on, let's go talk to him. She's, they're both so emotional.

BILL. You don't understand. It was a test, and she failed it. (*Pause.*) It's over.

(*HE shrugs. REN stares at him, confused. LIGHTS change.*)

Scene 9

Bill: A WHOLE DIFFERENT WORLD

REN and ED are in Ed's office.

ED. Hey! How's it going?

REN. Great. It's really—

ED. I'm glad you're here; I was gonna call you. You want to go do some editing?

REN. Yeah, sure.

ED. Also, we're going to have to stay late and take a look at next week's script. It's not quite working and Belinda's gonna leave the show, so I thought you and I could take a pass at it.

REN. Yeah, I just saw her. She's real upset.

ED. She's a talented girl; she'll be fine. Sometimes these things just don't work out.

REN. She really doesn't want to leave, Ed.

ED. I gave her a choice.

REN. Yeah, but, I, I think she didn't understand—see, I just think she's kind of insecure. This is all really new to her, I mean, we've all done it before, one way or another, and she's from a whole different world. That's all I think it is. And Sally really is—I know you guys have been through a lot together, but she's not been great to Belinda. You know how competitive women can be. She's—it's mostly when you're not around, but she gives her a hard time, and you know, it's clear to everyone else that it's because she's threatened, but how's Belinda supposed to know that? And she's good, everyone knows that, but she's just, she's figuring out how it all works, so she's a little ... I don't know. She makes some mistakes. But she loves the show, I know she loves being here, that's mostly what it is, I think.

(Pause.)

ED. So, what are you saying? Are you two sleeping together? Is that what you're telling me?

(Pause.)

REN. Would that be a problem?

ED. No! Jesus, no, I told you, I think she's great. I'm just—I mean, personally, I wouldn't be able to sleep with someone who's a better writer than I am. But hey, I think it's great. She'll land on her feet.

(THEY look at each other. LIGHTS change.)

Scene 10

Belinda: PRODUCER

BELINDA lies on Ren's bed. SHE holds a bottle of scotch, out of which SHE drinks. Beside the bed, there is a beautiful ten-speed bicycle, wrapped in red ribbon. REN enters. Pause.

REN. How are you?
BELINDA. Fine. How are you?
REN. Okay. Not so great. You know.

(SHE doesn't answer. HE sees the bicycle.)

REN. What's that?
BELINDA. It's a bicycle. Someone delivered it about
fifteen minutes ago.
REN. For me? I mean, it's ... for me?
BELINDA. Well, it's not for me.

*(Curious, REN crosses to look at it. HE finds a card and
starts to open it.)*

BELINDA. It's from Ed. He's making you a producer.

(Pause.)

REN. Yes. I know.
BELINDA. Oh. You saw Ed.
REN. Of course I saw him, Christ, what do you think,
I went over after you left and—
BELINDA. You went to see him? Oh. Did you talk
about me?

Escape

REN. Yes, as a matter of fact, we did. I told him this
was all a huge mistake.
BELINDA. You told Ed—*the* Ed—that he was making
a huge mistake?

(Pause. REN ~~does not answer~~.)

BELINDA. No, that's not what you told him. You told him *I* was making a huge mistake. By not begging for his love while he tromped all over me, I made a huge mistake. Thank you for your support. It means so much to me that you went in and explained that to your good friend Ed!

REN. Belinda—

BELINDA. Yeah, too bad it didn't work. I mean, you went in to beg for my job, and came out a producer. Poor Ren. You can't do anything right.

(Pause.)

REN. All you had to do was cry.

BELINDA. Fuck you. You think it's so fucking easy to cry for that creep, then you do it, you fucking woman.

(Pause.)

REN. I'm not going to talk to you right now. You're drunk.

BELINDA. Oh, that's rich. You can talk to a man who is completely insane well enough to get yourself that precious fucking producer button, but one drunken female has you tongue-tied.

REN. Jesus, you are—you know, you are just as bad as he is.

BELINDA. Not possible. No one's as bad as Ed. No one's as good as Ed. Only Ed exists, remember? You better remember, or he'll get you, too.

(SHE drinks from the bottle. HE reaches for it. SHE pulls away.)

REN. Give me the bottle.

BELINDA. You know what I think is interesting? You told me to fight. You said, he loves you. He wants you to fight for what you believe in. He wants you to fight for your script.

REN. Belinda—

BELINDA. You sent me in there, to fight, and I got fired, and now you're a producer. I find that very interesting.

REN. That's not what happened.

BELINDA. Isn't it? Then you tell me what happened. You—you tell me—

REN. Give me that. Would you give me that?

(SHE shoves him away.)

BELINDA. No. NO. Get your hands off me. Stay—just don't—

(Pause. REN sits on the bed.)

BELINDA. Why don't you tell me to go? Just tell me to go.

REN. I'm not going to do that. I don't understand any of this. I think I'm falling in love with you, and—it's not right what he did. I don't know what I'm going to do.

(HE rubs his eyes. SHE watches him. LIGHTS change.)

Scene 11

Bill: LOYALTY

STEVE, SALLY and BILL are in the writers' room.

SALLY. Well, I think it's definitely what needed to happen. She just wasn't fitting in. Already, you can feel how relieved everyone is.

I am relieved

BILL. I just don't know what we're gonna do for scripts now. I mean, she was a machine.

STEVE. I've got a lot of ideas. We can pick up the slack.

BILL. No, I know, I just—

SALLY. I think Ed always overrated her, frankly. I mean, she wrote fast, but we had to do a lot of work on her material.

STEVE. She wasn't funny. I didn't think. She just wasn't funny.

BILL. Well, she certainly wasn't loyal.

STEVE. And she just made everyone tense. I don't know *what* Ren sees in her.

SALLY. Oh, please. That's not going to last.

(REN enters, frazzled. SALLY is immediately sympathetic.)

SALLY. Ren! How are you?

REN. Oh, I'm fine. I'm sorry I'm late, I just, you know. Is Ed around?

BILL. He's at the network.

REN. Something going on?

BILL. You know. The usual shit. They're talking about the pickup.

REN. Oh, Jesus.

SALLY. (*Sympathetic.*) How's Belinda?

REN. She's fine. A little rattled.

SALLY. She'll be fine.

REN. Oh, yeah. She's already got, like, six job offers.

SALLY. (*Too polite.*) Really?

REN. Yeah, it's amazing how fast people hear somebody's available. You know, there's always work for someone who can write. She doesn't know what she's gonna do. You know, I don't think she's ready to just, dive into another show.

BILL. Fuck her.

SALLY. Bill.

BILL. No, I mean it. We give her her break, Ed hires her when she's nobody and now everybody wants her. Ed created her, and now she's off fielding offers from every shithead in town.

SALLY. Look. We're all upset by what happened—

BILL. No, look, I'm sorry, Ren, I know there's something going on between you two, but I'm not going to lie about how I feel.

REN. No, I know. I understand that.

BILL. I think a person should show a little loyalty. That's just how I feel.

REN. I agree, Bill.

BILL. I mean, Ed doesn't—Ed is not in this because he needs the power, or the money or anything. This is all a huge headache for him, and he has so much money, he doesn't have to do it anymore. He doesn't have to do anything unless he thinks it's going to benefit mankind.

REN. I know that.

BILL. So when she goes in there and tries to take over the show, how is he supposed to take that?

REN. I don't think that's what—

BILL. That's how it looked, all right? I mean, how else is he supposed to take it? And the next thing you know, she's calling her agents in. I don't think it's right. I think Ed deserves a little better than that.

REN. I understand what you're saying.

BILL. Do you?

(Beat . ED enters.)

ED. Hey, you hacks, how's it going?

BILL. Great!

ED. *(Sober.)* You guys got a minute?

(Pause.)

BILL. Sure. Sure! What's up?

ED. Well, you know, I know things have been a little tense around here lately, the numbers haven't been what we hoped and I know everyone's been pretty worried and wondering about what kind of life The Family of Mann has to look forward to. So I wanted everyone to know as soon as it happened. I just got back from the network and ... we've got our pickup.

(HE laughs. EVERYONE cheers.)

ED. I think this is a real vote of confidence for us from the network. They're under a lot of pressure to come up with shows that they really think are going to fly, and they're backing us a hundred percent. So I'd like everyone to just take a minute to feel good about all your hard work, and I think that we can now look forward to a lot of years together.

(EVERYONE cheers again.)

ED. And don't worry about the numbers; everybody at the network assures me that it's not going to matter. They're going to stand behind us no matter what, and we all know that there is someone out there who's eventually going to find us and say, thank god. Something real, and decent for a change.

(THEY all hug and applaud.)

SALLY Oh, isn't it wonderful?
BILL. Fantastic.
REN. That's great news, Ed.
ED. Yeah, it looks like we got a show for our new producer to produce! Now, get back to work. Hacks ... *(HE goes, laughing.)*
BILL. Well, how about that?
SALLY. What a relief!
STEVE. I wasn't worried.

(THEY all laugh.)

SALLY. Ren, we never congratulated you on your promotion. I think it's terrific.

REN. Thanks.

SALLY. Well, I guess if we're going for a whole season—

BILL. Hey, we're going longer than that. Seven years—

SALLY. Then we better get back to work!

BILL. All right! So what's Jim doing in this scene? Besides standing around with his fist up his ass.

STEVE. (*Snickers.*) You think that's physically possible?

BILL. It's the only way Jim's gonna get it.

STEVE. "Hey hey, Ralph! What are you doing?"

BILL. "I'm fucking myself, Norton! It's the wave of the future! You wanta watch?"

REN. "Hey hey hey hey!"

BILL. "Norton—you're the greatest!"

(BILL and STEVE laugh. REN tries to smile. CLARA enters. SHE wears her wings and passes out yellow sheets, menus and scripts.)

CLARA. Here are the lunch menus. Polaroids from wardrobe. Casting sheets. New second acts. Anything else?

BILL. Yeah, how would you like to give me a blow job?

(CLARA looks at him. The OTHERS laugh. The laughter dies out.)

CLARA. Actually, Bill, you know what I'd really like, is to cut it off and shove it down your throat.

(STEVE goes, "whoaaaa...." BILL stares at her, cold. SHE stares back. LIGHTS change.)

Scene 12

Clara: OUT IN THE COLD

BELINDA sits on a bench, smoking a cigarette. A bedraggled CLARA, still wearing her wings, approaches.

BELINDA. Hey. How's it going?

CLARA. Fine. Shitty, fine. (*SHE picks up the cigarettes from the bench and takes one.*) This city is, you know, man. This city is smoking. They're finally rioting over on Rodeo Drive.

BELINDA. They are?

CLARA. They should be. I mean, if I was gonna riot, that's what I'd do. I'd fucking burn Beverly Hills to the ground, that's what I'd do.

BELINDA. Bad day, huh?

CLARA. Please. Would you look at this place? Earthquakes. Fires. Riots! Floods! It's downright apocalyptic around here. The city of angels, my ass. This is Sodom and Gomorrah, and all this bad behavior is having an impact on the weather. The day of righteousness is at hand. Armageddon is starting at the corner of Wilshire and Fairfax, right down there in front of the May Company. I think it's already started.

(SHE smokes. BELINDA watches her.)

BELINDA. Clara?

CLARA. Yeah?

BELINDA. You've grown wings. You know that, don't you?

CLARA. You can see them?

(BELINDA nods.)

CLARA. Oh, thank god. Oh, Jesus. I thought I was losing my fucking mind, I got these major wings growing out of my back and nobody's even mentioned it! I mean, I go in that fucking room, and fucking Bill—I got fucking wings growing out of my back and he's asking me for a blow job!

BELINDA. He what?

CLARA. He asked me for a blow job. In front of everybody! Can you believe it?

BELINDA. What did you say?

CLARA. I told him I'd rather cut it off and shove it down his throat. Some angel I'm gonna make.

(THEY laugh.)

CLARA. You can see them? You actually see these things?

BELINDA. Yeah, they're pretty.

CLARA. You like them?

BELINDA. I think they're beautiful. Are they real?

CLARA. I guess! I mean, they kind of itch, you know? And they don t come off, which makes it real hard to get any sleep And sometimes, at night, they just move. On their own. They beat. They're anxious about something.

BELINDA. Me too.

CLARA. Yeah, me too.

BELINDA. Where'd they come from?

CLARA. I don't know. I was just sitting at my desk, right, everyone's screaming at me, and I start thinking about flying off, imagining what that would be like, to just float away. Fly off, into the sunset. The next thing I know, fucking wings. Growing out of my back.

(Beat.)

BELINDA. You imagined them. (*Pause.*) I can't, I can't imagine anything except buying a gun and shooting Ed, in an alley. (*Beat. Trying to collect herself.*) Clearly, wings are a much better way to go.

CLARA. Yeah. I think so. And I'm going to use them. I'm getting out of this town. I don't know why I stuck around this long. Unfinished business, I guess. You want to touch them? Go ahead. You can touch them.

BELINDA. No, I—no.

CLARA. It's okay.

(CLARA reaches over and takes Belinda's hand. SHE places it on one of her wings. BELINDA starts to cry. CLARA takes her in her arms and rocks her.)

(LIGHTS change.)

Scene 13

Ren: A GREAT OPPORTUNITY

The writers' room. REN is looking at scripts. BELINDA pokes her head in.

BELINDA. Hi.

REN. Belinda! What are—what are you doing here?

BELINDA. I just cleaned out my office. And, I was looking for you, actually. Everyone's gone, aren't they? I looked around, and—

REN. Yeah. Ed's over in his office. But everybody else left an hour ago. You're safe. (*Awkward pause. SHE looks around.*) So. What'd you do today?

BELINDA. I went to the tar pits.

REN. Again?

BELINDA. Yeah, you know, there's something about it I really find comforting. I think it's that dramatic recreation of the mastodon getting sucked into the tar. You know, the one you can see from the street. Her husband, and her little baby bellowing woefully at her from the bank. I find it kind of touching in a way that's unusual for Los Angeles.

REN. So how many times is that?

BELINDA. I don't know. Five or six.

REN. Just this week.

BELINDA. I've only been out of work this week. Give me a little more time, I may set a record. (*Pause.*) I bumped into Clara.

REN. You did?

BELINDA. Yeah.

REN. She had a kind of a run in with Bill. Did she tell you?

BELINDA. Actually, what she said was he asked her for a blow job. In front of a whole roomful of writers.

REN. Well, she gave as good as she got.

BELINDA. You notice anything different about her? About the way she looks or anything? Like, wings or anything?

REN. Wings?

BELINDA. Yeah, you know. Wings. (*Pause.*) Never mind. She says she's not coming back.

REN. Yeah. She made that pretty clear.

BELINDA. This city is smoking, you know? Clara told me that, at the tar pits, and I thought she meant that they were rioting again, but that's not it. I figured it out. She's talking about television.

REN. Really?

BELINDA. I think so. It's us that's burning. You know, we're, like, putting our lives into this cauldron, and turning up the heat so high—with the pressure, and the money, and the power, it's making us all white hot until our essence just burns away. You know, the best of us, the stuff that makes us human, it evaporates. And we're left with sitcoms. Maybe that's what all the smog is. It's not car exhaust. It's us, burning ourselves up.

REN. Belinda—

BELINDA. And then hanging there, in the air, like a disease. Like television. What is it? What are we becoming?

(*Pause. The door bursts open. ED enters.*)

ED. Hey, how's my new producer?

(Beat. HE takes her in.)

BELINDA. Ed.

REN. I was on my way over, Ed, she just stopped by for—

BELINDA. It's okay. *(Beat.)* I was picking up my stuff, Ed.

(Beat. THEY wait for Ed to respond.)

ED. *(To Ren.)* I'll be in my office, okay? Whenever you're ready. *(HE turns to go.)*

BELINDA. God, aren't you even going to let me say goodbye?

(HE stops and waits for her to continue. SHE crosses and holds out her hand. HE turns to Ren.)

ED. Whenever you're ready. No rush.

(HE goes. Beat. BELINDA looks at her hand.)

BELINDA. Whoa. I've been dissed. *(SHE laughs.)*

REN. Oh, shit. I have to go.

BELINDA. Oh, come on, Ren, relax. What's he gonna do if you don't hop, fire you? Pretty soon, he's not going to have any staff at all! *(SHE laughs.)*

REN. I don't have time for this! This is bad, don't you get it? It's bad that he saw me with you! *(Beat.)* I'm sorry.

BELINDA. (*Beat.*) Oh, no.

(*SHE looks at him. HE looks away.*)

REN. Look. I'm as sorry as anyone about what happened to you, but you have to understand, this is a great opportunity for me, and I need to protect myself here.

BELINDA. Don't do this.

REN. Don't—oh, that's great. Now *I'm* the villain.

BELINDA. No, you're not the villain, that's not— (*Regrouping.*) Look. I'm sorry I haven't been paying attention to what's going on with you, the position that you're in now, I—I've been so upset, it's like this whole place has poisoned me, and I'm trying to get myself back—

REN. This place is fine.

BELINDA. No, it's not, Ren, it's destroying people! And I think the longer you stay here, the more it infects you, and pretty soon you can't imagine anything else—

REN. What did you think you were going to find here? I mean, why is this all such a big surprise to you? I'm just a dumb jock from Illinois, and I knew it was going to be like this. Why didn't you just go back and tell Ed you were sorry?

BELINDA. Because he would do it again.

REN. Of course he would! He's the boss! That's what bosses do! I don't get why—how can you stand there and act like what's happened to you is so terrible? You had a good job, with people who admired you, and you gave it all up for pride—

BELINDA. Yes, I have pride—

REN. So the boss blows off steam in your direction, so what? He's under a lot of pressure. He's entitled. What's your problem?

BELINDA. Apparently my problem is I really do want people to be decent!

REN. It's a sitcom, Belinda! It's a fucking sitcom!

BELINDA. Well, this sitcom is a lie, and you're selling your soul to write it!

REN. Oh, no. That was never me. That's you, remember? I happen to like this show. I think it's funny, and smart, and *decent*. I'm proud to write for it, and I'm proud to work with Ed. I think I can learn a lot from him. I intend to try.

BELINDA. (*Pause*.) Ren. What are you—are we on feed? Is this being piped into Ed's office? (*SHE looks for the hidden mic.*) Ed-d-d ...

REN. I have to go. (*HE goes for his knapsack.*)

BELINDA. No. Please, listen to me. If you just go along with it all, you'll lose yourself.

REN. Look, I can't do this. Really, I can't fight with you anymore. I just can't. I have to go. (*HE heads for the door.*)

BELINDA. Hey. What are you and Ed doing? Are you rewriting my script?

REN. (*Beat*.) Yes, We are.

BELINDA. Well. Have a good time.

REN. Look. We all do what we have to do.

BELINDA. I know that! I know.

REN. I'll call you, okay?

BELINDA. Sure.

(HE goes. SHE sits, for a moment, looking at the room. From the darkness around him, the Mann family begins to take shape. THEY move in, whispering their lines. SHE turns.)

BELINDA. What? What do you want out of me? WHAT?

(THEY fall silent. SHE turns and looks at them as THEY surround her. SHE turns, finally, and looks at the script before her.)

BELINDA. Scene One: The Mann Family Kitchen.

(SHE looks at them, throws the script on the table, picks up her box and goes. The Family of Mann leans in to read the script.)

BLACKOUT

END OF PLAY

COSTUME LIST

BELINDA

Cream colored slacks
Black-striped tan slacks
Short-sleeved red shirt
Short-sleeved orange shirt
3 different vests
V-necked short-sleeved white T-shirt
White boxer shorts
Red ankle socks
White ankle socks
Black shoes
Tan shoes

REN

Blue jeans
Tan linen jacket
Light blue linen jacket
Short-sleeved maroon T-shirt
Short-sleeved navy blue T-shirt
Short-sleeved purple T-shirt
Short-sleeved gray pullover shirt
Red tank top
Grey drawstring sweatshorts
White tube socks
White sneakers

SALLY

Yellow silk sleeveless dress
Olive green jacket
Royal blue jacket
Yellow jacket
Tan silk skirt
Tan silk sleeveless blouse
Beige pumps
Pantyhose
Gold jewelry

ED

Tan jacket and pants
Grey silk jacket and pants
White turtleneck sweater
Tan turtleneck sweater
Black turtleneck sweater
Black shoes
Black socks

STEVE

Blue jeans
Red and grey striped shirt
Light blue long-sleeved shirt
Short-sleeved brown shirt with maroon collar
Short-sleeved turquoise T-shirt
Cowboy boots

BILL

Cream-colored pants
Light blue pants
4 different Hawaiian shirts
Black leather belt
Camel-colored shoes

CLARA

Short-sleeved white T-shirt
Short-sleeved white T-shirt with holes for harness wing
    hooks
Short-sleeved white T-shirt for under wing harness
Short-sleeved cream-colored T-shirt
Blue "Family of Mann" jacket
Blue shorts for under dress
Short denim overalls
Maroon shorts with white pattern
Short dress
Sneakers
Wings
Wing harness
Brown-framed sunglasses

<u>Sitcom clothes worn over street clothes</u>

SISSY

Black sweater with colored geometric designs
Fall of hair on comb

DAVE

Padded/fat sweater
Pipe

BUDDY

Grey, blue and red sweatjacket
Blue baseball cap

GINNY

Green & white striped robe
Fuschia headband
Pale green slippers

WILLY

Black and white plaid jacket
Black-framed eyeglasses

PROPERTY PLOT

I-1

6 chairs
6 scripts in binders
6 pencils
3 mugs
2-3 mugs (Belinda, Bill, Ren)
yellow pad

I-2
6 chairs
5 white scripts
5 pencils
box of mini-donuts
yellow pad
newspaper
Bill's binder
book of menus
mini-notebook on string
pen

I-3
Dave's sweater
Ginny's robe
4 chairs
newspaper
coffee pot
2 mugs
milk
Buddy's knapsack, coat, hat

Sissy's suitcase
Sissy's hair, coat

I-4
6 chairs
1 almost empty Coke can
Steve's mug
Bill's mug
6 white scripts (Bill's in binder)
6 pencils
yellow pad
bag of Chinese food: 3 large containers with broccoli, 6
    pairs of chopsticks, napkins
newspaper

I-5
2 chairs
blotter with phone
white script, yellow pad
Ed's mug
whiskey bottle, 2 glasses

I-6
armchair
cordless phone
remote control for TV

I-7
2 chairs
blotter with phone
bottle of single malt whiskey
2 whiskey glasses

I-8
5 chairs
white script
white script, yellow pad
stack of yellow paper with numbers
several Polaroid snapshots
stack of scripts

I-9
3 chairs
flowers in paper
vase
tea table with service
blotter with phone
stack of scripts

I-10
couch
1 chair
knapsack
multi-colored script
desk blotter with phone

I-11
4 chairs
sports section of paper
glass of milk
"Help Wanted" section of paper
cookie sheet
"fresh baked" cookies
oven mitt

spatula
plate

I-12
5 chairs
empty coffee maker
knapsack
cookie box
2 stacks of orange paper
2 stacks of white paper
2 pencils
misc. scripts, papers
handbag
2 Diet Cokes
Ed's mug

I-13
4 chairs
2 empty (used) rocks glasses
2 glasses of scotch with stirrers
handbag

I-14
6 chairs
4 white scripts, Bill's binder
3 pencils
5 legal pads
Ed's mug
refrigerator

I-15
5 chairs

cigarettes
lighter
Belinda's mug
knapsack

II-2
pillows
catalogues
white script
pencil

II-3
4 chairs
Dave's sweater
Willy's jacket, glasses
Sissy's hair, coat
Buddy's hat, coat
5 multi-colored scripts: Buddy, Willy (+white from II-4),
   Dave, Sissy, Bill's in binder)
10 salmon-colored sheets
wrench
cigarettes
lighter
drinking glass
2 bottles/cans of beer

II-4
4 chairs
Sally's mug
white script(s)
Steve's 2 scripts, salmon pages
1 white script in binder

handbag
knapsack

II-5
2 chairs
blotter with phone
armchair
videocassettes and covers
paper work
pencil
several Polaroids
white script

II-6
2 chairs
full tea service: tea pot, cup
armchair
Dave's sweater
Ginny's robe
Buddy's robe
Sissy's robe
white script

II-7
2 chairs
blotter with phone
white script, pencil
all orange script (proofs)
tea cup

II-8
couch
1 chair
blotter with phone
handkerchief

II-9
2 chairs
grapefruit
napkins
trash can

II-10
4 chairs
3 white scripts
knapsack
stack of yellow papers with numbers
book of menus
several Polaroids
second acts

II-12
cigarettes and lighter
paper cup with touch of water

II-13
4 chairs
Bill's mug
Bill's binder
cigarette and lighter
tea tray with tea pot, cup, saucer, spoon
2 multi-colored scripts

II-14
4 chairs
stack of scripts (top one has cover taped open)
knapsack
box of office accessories